W. H. HUDSON

By the same Author

THRENODY FOR DORMICE

THE DAY OF THE ROSE

DEER'S CRY (published by the Fortune Press)

ALL SOULS (published by Faber & Faber)

W. H. HUDSON AT THE AGE OF 27

GREAT NATURALISTS SERIES
Editor: R. M. LOCKLEY

W. H. HUDSON

By

RUTH TOMALIN

LONDON:
H. F. & G. WITHERBY LTD.

First published in 1954 by
H. F. & G. Witherby Ltd.
5 Warwick Court, London w.c.1.

Acknowledgements

THE AUTHOR's most grateful thanks are due to Sir Eugen Millington-Drake, K.C.M.G., Founder and President of Hudson House and Chairman of Canning House Library Committee, for the use of the Millington-Drake W. H. Hudson Collection which now forms part of the Canning House Library, 2 Belgrave Square; to Miss Jean Wagstaff, Assistant Librarian at Canning House, for her invaluable help; and to the staff of the British Museum Reading Room; to the Royal Society for the Protection of Birds and Messrs. J. M. Dent & Sons, for permission to make use of copyright material from the following works of W. H. Hudson: *Far Away and Long Ago, Idle Days in Patagonia, Birds in London, The Purple Land, Afoot in England, Nature in Downland, El Ombú, Marta Riquelme, Green Mansions, A Shepherd's Life*; three poems, "A Lullaby", "Gwendoline" and "A London Sparrow"; two papers, "On the Birds of the Rio Negro of Patagonia" and "Swallows of Buenos Aires", published in the Proceedings of the Zoological Society of London; letters of W. H. Hudson to Dr. Spencer Fullerton Baird of the Smithsonian Institution, Washington, and to Dr. P. L. Sclater of the Zoological Society of London (published by Cornell University Press under the title, "Letters on the Ornithology of Buenos Aires", edited by David R. Dewar); and letters to Violet Hunt, Morley Roberts, R. B. Cunninghame Graham, Edward Garnett and an anonymous correspondent;

to the Smithsonian Institution, Washington, for permission to reproduce a photograph from their files;

to Messrs. A. P. Watt & Son and the executors of the late Mr. Morley Roberts for permission to quote three passages from "W. H. Hudson: A Portrait", by Morley Roberts;

to Messrs. Hamish Hamilton and Mr. Stephen Spender for permission to quote a passage from "World Within World", by Stephen Spender:

to Messrs. Longmans Green & Co. and Prof. G. M. Trevelyan, O.M., C.B.E., for permission to quote a passage from "English Social History" by G. M. Trevelyan;

and, for their courtesy in sending letters and information, to: Mr. D. H. Aaron, Mr. Louis Adeane, Mr. Edward A. Armstrong, Mr. E. F. Bozman, Sir Sydney Cockerell, Mr. Philip Gosse, Mr. Robert Hamilton, the Rev. F. W. Potto Hicks, Mrs. Elsa Inwood, Miss Daphne Lawes, Mr. William J. Mead, Mr. James Fairweather Milne, Mrs. Naomi Milton, Mr. Eric Norris, Mme Victoria Ocampo (Buenos Aires), Mr. James L. Palmer, Miss Louise M. Pearson (the Smithsonian Institution, Washington), the directors Penguin Books Ltd., Mr. Omar S. Pound, Mr. Guy Rawlence, Mr. Percy Redfern, Lady (Alice) Rothenstein, the Hon. Victoria Sackville-West, C.H., Mr. H. Sargeant (Portsmouth City Librarian), Mrs. Tatyana Schmoller, Mrs. Shepherd, Mr. G. B. Stratton (Librarian, The Zoological Society of London), Mrs. Helen Thomas, Mr. Masao Tsuda (Tokio) and Mr. R. L. Watson.

Contents

		PAGE
Prologue: THE SPLENDOUR IN THE GRASS		9
CHAPTER		
I.	PAMPAS BOYHOOD	18
II.	STUDIES: FOR LIFE AND DEATH	36
III.	THE BIRD-COLLECTOR	49
IV.	THE STONE FOREST	72
V.	A GARRET IN WESTBOURNE PARK	95
VI.	A KINGDOM TO HIMSELF	110
VII.	THE TIME REMAINING	129
	BIBLIOGRAPHY	141

The Splendour in the Grass

ONE AUGUST day in the hot summer of 1899 a
man who had walked for several hours over the
Sussex downs near Lewes sat down on the grass
to rest. A warm wind was blowing the seed-heads
from many discs of flat dwarf thistles on the turf, and
as he watched the yellow-tinted fleeces drifting through
the air there came to him a memory of summers half
a century before; when as a boy he had lain beneath
another sky, while thistledown floated above him from
tall seeding thickets.

Everyone has known what it is to leave behind the
world of a young child, peopled by giants and wooded
by towering weeds, and to enter the dwindled world
of a grown person; but for this man the change had
been far intensified. His early years were passed in a
country where a "thistle year" made dense jungles,
not only higher than himself but higher than his father
—as high as the orchard trees, and set with huge
purple flowers and with spines like daggers. Through
days of burning sunlight or dark hot nights he had
seen their white gossamers rise and fall like bubbles
on the breeze, or whirled in blizzards before a pampas
wind.

To the end of his long life, Hudson was to be haunted
by this shining memory—by the blue flames of the
thistle flowers, by his sense of happiness and dreaming
indolence as he gazed at the moving thistledown, by

its gleam in the moonlight, by the excitement of
urging a nervous horse breast-high through ghostly
drifts of whiteness, and by the triumph of galloping
over level plains and hearing the crackle of withered
stems "like the bones of perished foes" when autumn
rains and hurricane winds had levelled the jungles
again.

He was six years old then, master of his own pony,
and able to ride out over the green plain that travelled
to the horizon, where the blue dome of the sky rested
on the grass; a world full of beauty, terror and strangeness in which he was free to run wild.

When rain fell, the grass shone vivid emerald under
flashing pools of water, and earth and leaves were
drenched with a sweetness that made him race and roll,
ecstatic as a puppy. In the first days of spring, the turf
was covered with yellow stars of blossom like celandines,
holding him spellbound to watch them glimmering in
the wind. In summer, when the flowers had shrivelled,
myriads of spiders' webs silvered the grass, so that the
setting sun cast a wide beam to his feet as though it
were shining across water. Like water too the bright
air above the plain danced and shimmered in waves,
from early spring through the parched summer, when
the sluggish rivers failed in the marshes. In autumn
again the brown grass was brilliant green, and white
clouds ran before the winds that swept the leaves from
the home plantation.

Trees were rare on the pampas, and to the child this
little woodland and orchard were marvellous. The old
peach trees every August broke into a cloud of rose-pink
blossom, between the green earth and blue sky, and
thousands of yellow finches sang from the flowering
branches, their long trills streaming across the sense

like a vision of straight white rain to the eye. Gnarled quince trees twisted themselves into curious shapes, and the paradise tree and tree of heaven threw deep shadows under the hot sun; while in the dark tunnels of mulberry-walks a child could feast like a wild bird. A willow drew him in summer to watch a nesting scissor-tail battling with hawks in the air above, a grove of poplars to see the golden siskins building, and the white acacias to watch their leaves trembling by moonlight. Even the black acacia, armed with vicious thorns, tempted him again and again for a glimpse of sapphire-blue eggs in a Guira cuckoo's nest, or the pale green eggs of the yellow-billed cuckoo. All winter he would wander in the plantation to look for signs of spring, lingering quietly while he watched the sky through the branches and the few wintering swallows wheeling in the air, touching the bark with his fingers, breathing the scent of damp moss and of violets springing under the poplar roots; his thoughts all the while lighting up his mind like candles, and his senses alert for every sound or movement in the grass.

A great red willow was his favourite tree, shared with a peregrine falcon in a lonely part of the wilderness. Here, from the highest boughs, he could gaze out over the grass and dream of taking wing from his perch and soaring in the air like a seagull: or like the crested screamer, which was heavier than himself, and yet could launch itself from the earth to float for hours at ease in the upper air.

The wish for wings sprang naturally from his passion for birds. The voices of birds, their joyful lives in the sky and trees, their colours and the sound of their wings, filled him with delight. Emerald parakeets flocked among the peach blossoms, humming-birds glittered in the garden over blue morning-glories and scarlet four-o'clock blossoms, and tyrant-birds, shining in black and scarlet, came south in spring from their tropical forests. Rainbow-feathered parrots, eagles, golden owls, swans, plovers and purple troupials flashed in and out among yellow lilies, scented mauve and pink verbenas and violet-flowered dwarf palms, and over the fields of blue alfalfa with their flocks of sipping butterflies.

More splendid were the birds of the lagoons and flowery meres—the blue ibis that bred among the sedges of the furthest lagoon, the storks, crested screamers, beautifully marked black and red jacana, black and white stilts, and roseate spoonbills with their peach-blossom colouring and delicately balanced flight. Wild geese from the Magellan Straits, swans and herons, painted snipe and dazzling white egrets, rose-billed ducks and blue-winged teal nested among the sedges, dabbling and flashing across the shallows where the dark leaves and yellow trumpets of the *camaloté* floated, thick as mimulus in an English brook. At his first visit he was only just old enough to walk the miles across the plain, skirting thistle patches and struggling through waist-high grass. The small naturalist was rewarded, however, by seeing a flock of rare flamingos upon a distant lake; and to his eyes the great birds, with their wide-spread crimson wings, were marvellous as a host of angels troubling the flooded waters of the stream. Many times in his youth he was to see flamingos, but never again with the awe he felt at that moment.

Beside the extravagant beauty of his world, the child accepted its reptiles and venomous spiders, wild cattle and savage birds of prey: all the perils and hazards of a land where a baby, put to sleep on a rug in the shade, might be attacked by a deadly snake; where a boy climbing a peach-tree to steal an egg from the nest of a vulture might find himself forced to descend violently in fear of his life; or where, thrown by his pony on the open plain, he might be devoured by a wild sow, "bones and boots included", so that only a rag of his clothes would remain for the searchers to find.

Yet serpents, from which he was warned to run, fascinated as much as they frightened him. At night, as he lay awake in the darkness, imagination tortured him with visions of snakes gliding and coiling about his bed; but by day, finding a sloughed snakeskin, he would handle and play with it, delighting in the silken smoothness under his fingers, its soft rustle that almost made him start with fear, the silvery colour and the illusion of danger from its likeness to the living creature. Soon the charm of serpents, their pale green or blue and crimson skins, their poisoned fangs and the sense of worship roused in him by their beauty and mystery, sent him in search of them as eagerly as he hunted for birds or flowers.

There was one patch of sterile clay in the plantations where thickets of weeds struggled to grow, and here, with a child's perversity, he would idle on hot days among the ugly withered stems. One blazing December day he heard a rustle and saw a strange black snake, six feet long, flow past into the weeds. Though trembling with horror, he could not keep away from the place, and at last he again saw the snake glide by him and pour itself into a hole. Now he began to haunt the weeds and to wait outside the den for it to reappear, but he saw no sign of it until, going to look at a cluster of bats in a mulberry tree some way off, he felt a pressure on his foot and looked down to see the snake moving slowly across his instep. The child kept still, his first thrill of fear and aversion quickly gone; and although he never saw it again, he was left with the feeling which he kept all his life—that the snake had not harmed him because he had watched for it, not with hatred or to kill it, but in a reverent and gentle spirit.

On summer nights he could hear the clans of commoner snakes moving beneath the floors of the old house, where they seemed to hold long hissing conversations, "a long sibilation followed by distinctly heard ticking sounds, as of a husky-ticking clock, and after ten or twenty or thirty ticks another hiss, like a long expiring sigh, sometimes with a tremble in it as of a dry leaf swiftly vibrating in the wind . . . and so it would go on, demand and response, strophe and antistrophe. . . ."

In winter, when the serpents slept coiled together in silence, the nights echoed to a sound still eerie yet less subtle: a roar of croaking from the marshes close to the house. Here, in the flooded water-courses, swarms of great toad-like amphibians preyed on the smaller toads, and chanted in a raging chorus that ranged through every key.

But in the autumn, as he listened on still moonlit nights, the boy heard a different drumming that stirred him to the heart—the sound of wings in the air, and the ringing of bird cries from the high darkness where swans and swallows, wild geese, whistling duck and glossy ibis, whimbrels and rails streamed past. Day after day and night after night the flocks crossed the sky, swept from their summer haunts by the urge of migration. They seemed to him like the thistledown which was first loosed from its husk by a soft breeze, then blown lightly from one resting-place to another on a wandering breeze, and at last swirled away on the surge of a rising gale.

The birds returned in spring so quietly that little was heard of their approach. He waited to hear the calls of lapwings, the pipit's spring song, the cuckoo's note; and as the leaves unfolded in the poplar grove, he learned that to live with poplars was to have the noise of flowing water always in his ears.

The grass was full of strange voices—the shrill outcry of pampas rats, alarm cries of deer, bubbling talk of guinea-pigs, metallic hammer-notes of ibis, the crash of thunderstorms, pipe of grasshoppers, and flitter of dragon-flies. Mingled with these were all its vivid scents—the sweetness of young poplar leaves, peach blossom, violets; the scent of locust blossom and the flowers of the paradise tree, of deer, sheep and skunks; of young grass, pungent swamps and perfumed white verbenas; the golden perfume of the small lily, the Virgin's Tears, for which he hunted in the tall grasses, trying to carry the fragile blossoms home to his mother before their petals fell; and the bitter tang of the fennel thicket where he liked to loiter, as children have done all over the world and in each generation, crushing and tasting the leaves of the herb,

> Snipping the tips and shrivelling
> The shreds at last onto the path, perhaps
> Thinking, perhaps of nothing, till he sniffs
> His fingers and runs off. . . .[1]

[1] Edward Thomas.

Intriguing as rare birds were the men and women seen in these earliest years—a beggar on horseback, a young murderer tied in the barn, a strange little girl, white-skinned and black-haired, flying past him on her pony; and ancient nightwatchmen, walking the city streets with their long cloaks and lanterns, crying the hours in tones that moved him as much as the sounds of snake and upland plover at home on the open plain.

The boy did not seek out other people, even other children, for companionship. Often he escaped from his brothers to steal away by himself; and when his mother followed him to see what could be wrong, she found him perhaps hidden among the high weeds of the orchard, watching a pair of scarlet flycatchers building their nest of lichen in a peach tree, and so absorbed that he never heard her coming or knew when she left him to his chosen happiness.

She understood his feelings: that, born like herself with the searching instincts of a naturalist, he was already living a secret life of discovery and delight. To touch soft mullein leaves or hot smooth eggs in a nest, to see a splash of scarlet verbenas in green grass, to hear the voices of mocking birds, to taste honey and peaches, to smell rain and tansy and lilies, touched him to a response that had its roots in her own love of life and of every living thing.

This was the country which the wanderer saw in his reverie while he lay on the English downs, watching the minute puffs of thistledown and remembering the giants of the past.

But he remembered also that the great bird-flocks of his childhood had been wiped out, the lagoons drained where he had seen their coloured shadows, the wild-flowers gone, the marshes ploughed and set with field

16

crops, and the land inhabited by strangers. He told himself, "I am glad to think I shall never revisit them. I shall finish my life thousands of miles removed from them, cherishing to the end in my heart the image of a beauty which has vanished from earth."

Chapter I

Pampas Boyhood

Twenty-five gigantic trees, each trunk so mighty that five men could not encircle it, made a land-mark beside a long, low farm-house in the province of Florencia Varela, Buenos Aires, on the pampas of La Plata. The house took its name, "The Twenty-five Ombús", from this line of strange ever-green trees.

Slow-growing and long-lived, with their spongy, wood and dense glossy leaves, they were already a hundred years old when there played in their branches a child whose friends, another century later, would journey to gaze at the last of the grove still standing beside the scarcely altered house.

In this modest dwelling Daniel and Caroline Hudson made their first home some years after they landed in South America. Though built of brick, with tiled roof and verandah, the three-roomed house can have seemed little better than a shack to these settlers from a conventional New England background; but, having arrived with little capital and a hopeful spirit in this young country where great fortunes were to be made, they would probably accept it as a temporary shelter until the foundations of their success were laid and they could find or build a better home.

Like the trees, it was already old, and was said to be haunted by the pitiful ghost of a negro slave whom a former owner had had beaten to death. It stood at

18

the top of a slope by a road running south toward Chascomus from Buenos Aires, the capital city, which had not yet spread across the plain to change the lonely character of the place. That stretch of road was known locally by the phrase, "De la Casa de Teja a la Harquetadura" ("From the tiled house to the bend").

Daniel Hudson, whom his son remembered with affection and exasperation, as a man of "shining defects", would be at this time in his late twenties. Son of a Devon man from Clyst Hyden, near Exeter, who had emigrated to America, and of an Irish mother, he had been born on May 1st, 1804 at Marblehead, Massachusetts. His wife, Caroline Augusta Kimble, a descendant of a *Mayflower* immigrant, was a few months younger, having been born at Berwick, Maine, on October 10th, 1804.

As a young married man Daniel had worked in a brewery, and here, while climbing or running among tiers of barrels, perhaps in some feat of thoughtless daring in keeping with his character, he had fallen and injured his back. Recovering from this mishap, he found himself threatened with tuberculosis, and the decision followed to leave for a happier climate, and the open-air life of a pampas farmer. Perhaps, too, the young couple found the spiritual climate of their surroundings too austere. Daniel Hudson, with his tolerant *laissez-faire* temperament (the gift of his mother's race) breaking out only on occasion into a flash of energy, anger or recklessness, might well feel out of his element in a formal Quaker community; while his wife, with her deep faith, and in spite of the strictness of her religious upbringing, possessed a nature so little rigid, so generous and warmhearted, that in La Plata the poorest among her Catholic Spanish neighbours were to love and rely on her as "the mother of us all".

The small estancia of "The Twenty-five Ombús", a strip rather less than a mile wide and extending about four and a half miles back into the grassy wilderness, was bought by Daniel Hudson in April 1837 from Tristan Valdez, a brother-in-law of Juan Manuel Rosas, the famous dictator of Buenos Aires. The couple by this time had two sons, three-year-old Daniel, born after their arrival in the Argentine, and Edwin, aged one. Their purchase of the ranch was followed in 1839 by the birth of a daughter, Carolina Louisa. Then, on St. Dominic's Day, August 4th, 1841, a third son was born there, and, since they lived in too remote a place for a clergyman to visit them, the baby was taken to Buenos Aires to be christened William Henry.

Within a few years a fourth son, Albert Merriam, and another girl, Mary Ellen, completed the family, and became the childhood companions of the little boy who was to distinguish himself in later years as W. H. Hudson.

Growing up in the crowded farmhouse, under the shadow of the strange trees, William had received before he was five years old a few vivid impressions of this early life which would remain always imprinted on his mind. Most stirring of these scenes was the evening homecoming of the cattle, bellowing and clouding the green plain with dust, and the cries of herdsmen galloping behind in the sunset light. He could recall, too, his mother's face as she sat before the house at sunset, her book on her lap, smiling as she watched the children playing on the green turf. At the back, a grassy slope ran down to a wide stream, a tributary of the River Plate, and they would run scampering along the banks under the red willows, shouting with delight to smell the pungent sodden earth. Sheep as well as cattle were bred on the Hudson land, and a lame sheepdog figured in these glimpses, partly because of his protective air and tolerance of childish teasing, but also in a rueful light: William having fallen from his back and broken his leg at the age of four, while taking a riding-lesson from his brothers. There was also a gentle, white-whiskered giant known as Captain Scott, who brought the little ones sugar-plums and took them fishing, and so became something of a hero to William; and—most curious of all human beings he met with, either then or in later life—a wandering hermit weighed down with "penances", like medieval tortures, for some unknown crime.

But here the images faded, leaving only the remembrance of a midwinter journey across the plain to a new home which was to see his happiest years: a long childish idyll in which the field naturalist began unconsciously to grow within the joyful "little wild animal running about on its hind legs"; while, deeper still, slept the embryo artist who would learn to interpret the feelings and adventures of both.

To most adult eyes, however, there would be little of the idyll in the situation of the family, isolated in a strange land among savage civil wars and feuds; the father losing such struggles as he made against ill-luck or his own lack of initiative; the mother using all her strength to make for her children the kind of cultivated home life which she and her husband must have known; and the children themselves, as they grew older, becoming aware of their poverty and lack of education. Yet William and his brothers and sisters were happy in their parents, who gave them laughter and freedom in a century that was generally severe to the young, sympathy with their widely different natures, and a precious sense of security in spite of the cruelty and bloodshed surrounding them.

The same trustful easy-going fatalism, half-amused, and perhaps half-perverse, which prevented Daniel Hudson from succeeding in his business undertakings, and even from taking the trouble to make his property legally secure, made him also brave to the point of foolhardiness. During one of the appalling pampas thunderstorms, he was seen standing coolly on the dizzy look-out point at the top of the bar, spy-glass in hand, searching the distance for missing horses. On another occasion, during the rebellion of 1852, his coolness actually saved the lives of his family. The soldiers of Rosas' defeated army were in retreat, killing and looting as they went, but in spite of neighbours' warnings the Hudson house remained with doors and windows open and no means of defence. The only precaution taken was to drive the horses into a plantation out of sight. When a troop of men arrived, shouting for horses, Daniel declared that he had none to give them, and stood smiling quietly before the menace of a drawn sword, until the intruders withdrew, convinced that he must have a strong guard behind him to behave so calmly. This behaviour was all the more striking to the children because of the terror shown by the only other man in the house, a visitor: and also because they heard later that, on the same day, an unfortunate young officer had fled for protection to the house of a relative who was a magistrate in the district, but had been given up by the old man to be murdered, to save his own family from attack.

The new estancia, known as "The Acacias", was

situated in the province of Chascomus, about fifty-five miles from Buenos Aires city. Here Daniel farmed sheep and also became the district storekeeper. In the front rooms of this house, which faced the road, the country people traded their own produce—wool, hides and horse-hair, tallow and cheeses—and bought their groceries, household goods, clothes, saddlery, even coffins.

While their father applied himself to these new ventures, and the children explored the orchard, plantation and gardens, Caroline Hudson attacked the chaos from which she was to make another home. The great derelict brick house was surrounded by barns, kitchen, bakery, dairy, thistlewood-piles and offal-heaps, all in an appalling state of dirt and disorder, and overrun by vermin, fleas, snakes, spiders, and hordes of enormous rats that swarmed from the dry moat and rubbish-pits, even scuttling over the children's beds at night.

To this task she brought the pioneer spirit of courage and resource, proving herself equal to life in a country where nature gave lavishly with one hand and dealt destruction with the other: where giant thistles fattened the stock and gave mountains of dry fuel, but spoiled the taste of cow's milk and threatened the homestead with disastrous fires; where hot summers supplied her kitchen with bushels of apples, pears and peaches for pickling or sweet preserves, melons, pumpkins, and every kind of vegetable, but were followed by months of searing drought, succeeded in their turn by storms which brought floods, fearful lightning, and great hailstones that could kill a child or a sheep, cut garden crops to pieces and ravage the fruit trees. A boy of six could be sent out to gather unlimited wild-fowl eggs, a boy of ten could shoot wild duck or pigeons for the pot, and one ostrich egg would make an omelette for an entire household; but the first word a little child learned must be "ku-ku"— "dangerous"—a warning cry uttered by the nurse or mother as he was snatched away from snake or spider. Again, when the older children were late in coming home, she would have an appalling catalogue of dangers to dread from birds, beasts and reptiles, as well as the ordinary hazards of boyhood in climbing trees, swimming and riding; together with any further mischief that might have befallen them in running wild among gaucho herdsmen.

So William, growing to independence in that wonderful sixth year, found himself beginning to lead three lives at once: the secret life of the naturalist, the active one of games, lessons, squabbles, practical jokes, and ambitious schemes in a circle of six high-spirited children, and the life of the small native learning to preserve himself in a savage wilderness where violence was commonplace.

On his first visit to Buenos Aires, he found the streets full of marvels as he wandered about by himself. The great Plata river, wide as a sea, where coloured washerwomen spread out their linen on the beach, gabbling away together like flocks of waterbirds by a lagoon; the parading men and women of fashion, and, equally engaging to a child, policemen with their blue coats and swords; the paved courtyard of the house where he and his mother were staying with friends, the scarlet cardinal bird in its cage, the romantic orange groves, the thundering of horses' hooves and springless carts all enchanted him.

One moment stood out clearly from among these new impressions. Stealing up the stairway of the great city church, William had his first experience of orchestral music. To the child from the plain, who had never heard any instrument but a guitar, this music was a revelation, charming him to a deep and almost painful emotion.

It was in this year also that there came an incident which affected him more than any other in his childhood, and left a lifelong mark. An old dog, a much-loved family pet, had died; and the children watched his burial under a peach tree in the orchard. It occurred to their stagestruck schoolmaster, rather in the spirit of Mr. Fairchild and other instructors then in favour, to "improve the occasion". Looking round at their sober faces, he observed, "That's the end. Every dog has his day, and so has every man; and the end is the same for both. We die like old Caesar, and are put into the ground and have the earth shovelled over us."

These comments, the first to bring home to him the idea of annihilation, threw William into a piteous state of grief and horror. After some days he could bear it no longer, and appealed to his mother for reassurance, at the same time dreading that she would confirm the terrible words. Her answer, in which she tried to explain to his childish understanding the idea of the survival of the spirit, filled him for that moment with relief, as though he were a prisoner set free from torture; but he never again lost his hatred of the thought of death, nor resolved his doubts of the religious teaching with which his mother tried after this crisis to help him. The sight of cattle being slaughtered daily—brutal sport as well as necessity to the gauchos—cruelly underlined his fears; and the death that same year of Margarita, a beautiful young girl acting as nurse to the smaller children, still further increased his distress.

It was not any morbid strain in William which produced these feelings, but a love of living and of beauty which was the keynote of his existence. Now began his solitary rides over the plain to look for new birds in other plantations. This passion for birds, and his excitement when he discovered a strange one, amused his family, and the little fellow now and then found himself teased for his enthusiasm. He spent hours one spring day trying to catch doves, as he had been advised, by putting salt on their tails. Another time, his elder brothers snared a common cow-bird and dyed its tail red in the hope of deceiving him. When Edwin had the idea, a few years later, of starting a family paper to which all were to contribute, William was at once commanded to write something about birds, this being already his special subject; and in later years he thought it unfortunate that the idea of the paper came to nothing, since it would have taught him to make notes of everything he saw.

Three attempts were made during William's boyhood to provide schooling for the children. Their first master, Mr. Triggs, arrived soon after the move to "The Acacias", when William was not yet six, and the change from freedom to the confinement of the schoolroom was painful. Mr. Triggs was a middle-aged Englishman who detested children, but who had taken to teaching as the easiest way to support himself in that country without undue effort. Loving comfortable living, good talk and good books, the Hudson household suited him perfectly, and for a long time he made himself agreeable to the grown-up members, who were delighted with him. He had been at one time an actor, and proved himself a brilliant impersonator, reading Dickens to the family every evening and interpreting each character. Once he played a wonderful masquerade, arriving disguised as an old Scots dame visiting from a distant farm. So well did he sustain the part that the children actually sat for an hour at the tea-table, their eyes fixed on his face and their ears drinking in the "old lady's" scandalous gossip, without detecting their schoolmaster. In the schoolroom, however, he was a different man—not a genial entertainer, but a short-tempered tyrant. Forbidden to use a cane, which to William's father and mother would have been a crime, he had to vent his irritation by pinching his pupils' ears, and they soon learned to detest him in return.

However, he began at last to spend his weekends in drinking rum at another farm, and one Monday morning, losing control of his temper, he snatched up a horsewhip and lashed out blindly at the children. He was at once dismissed; for the Hudsons, who never struck and seldom scolded their children, could not overlook such a lapse into cruelty.

For some time the four younger children were given lessons by their mother, while the two elder boys, already impatient of schoolmasters, studied by themselves. Edwin was delighted, however, to hear that a new master had been found who was qualified to help him with mathematics, his chief interest. The newcomer was Father O'Keefe, an Irish priest. The children soon found that he erred rather on the side of gentleness and leniency, expecting little in the way of work, himself forgetting school hours unless reminded, and glad of any excuse to give his pupils a holiday and go fishing. The promised coaching in mathematics proved shortlived, Edwin reporting in disgust that Father O'Keefe "knew as much of the

infinitesimal calculus as a gaucho", and adding with
laughter that he only wished he had pretended also
to be an expert boxer.

Edwin relieved his feelings by forming the young
ones into a regiment of lancers, which would charge
after the master as he set out on his rides, hurling cane
lances at his horse's heels. The horse at times kicked
out angrily under the lances, but Father O'Keefe,
deep in reverie, never turned his head nor seemed to
realise that he was playing the harried foe in retreat.
So the indolent régime continued, until the priest,
secretive and pleasantly vague to the last, departed
to attend to his own affairs.

The third was by far the finest teacher, but his stay
was brief. He was a lively young man, with some
knowledge of science, a mathematician, fencer and
boxer. He was also well-read, a musician and a
linguist, and for the first time William began to take
an interest in lessons, stung by the master's zeal and
his hearty scorn of such ignorant "young barbarians".
Then he too broke down and returned to the drunken-
ness which had already cost him his profession.

The one English school in Buenos Aires had a bad
name as a crowded, unhealthy house, and no money
could be spared to send the boys further away. Their
parents, too, imagined that their lives would probably
lie in farming on the pampas, and that formal education would not be greatly missed. Only Edwin refused
to accept this idea of his future, setting himself to follow
his mathematical bent, in spite of delays and difficulties in
obtaining books and instruments: giving up all outdoor
sports, his place as family spinner of tales, and all reading
for amusement, until by sheer determination he had
his way and left to continue his education abroad.

This remarkable boy had a great influence on William. Five years his senior, and masterful to the point of tyranny in his dealings with younger brothers, Edwin could never be as close a companion to William as the youngest boy, Albert. These two stood together in defiance of the lordly Edwin, who poured scorn on their childish ideas, took the lead in their bathing, fishing and egg-hunting rambles, and made them his unwilling opponents in fencing and boxing practice. The trio were nearer to equality and friendship, however, after an episode when Edwin made up his mind that he should learn to defend himself with a knife—the gaucho weapon—and persuaded nine-year-old William and the smaller Albert to join against him in a fight with butchers' knives. It was William in the end who was wounded, receiving a deep cut on the arm from which the blood poured out; but, proud of his brother's rare praise at his courage, he refused to tell his elders the reason for his bandaged arm. From that time, in gratitude, Edwin became less domineering.

William's ambition since he was seven had been to carry a gun and shoot birds; but Edwin who had appointed himself armourer to the household, told him he must wait until his tenth birthday, and content himself meanwhile with following his elder brother to retrieve his birds or hold his pony. About this time, however, an old family friend gave William a set of pen-and-ink drawings which Edwin coveted, and a bargain was struck. The pictures were handed over, and William found himself the possessor of a silver-mounted single-barrel fowling-piece, and passed a brief test by bringing down a pigeon in the plantation. So began the career as a wild-fowler which was to continue as long as he lived in South America, a practice in strange contrast to his preaching of later years.

When another war came in the following year, and lawless troops threatened the district, Edwin, disapproving of his father's casual ways, undertook to prepare the defence of the house. Powder and shot were scarce, and, though not restricting his own shooting, Edwin saw to it that William should not be wasteful. He also cleaned a strange collection of weapons—ancient muskets, horse-pistols and fowling pieces—and set his young brothers to work at melting down lead and making bullets in bullet-moulds of different sizes. The three boys were laughed at for their pains, and, after turning out hundreds of bullets, they were disappointed to find that the danger had passed without their firing a shot.

This delight in shooting might seem surprising in a child who not only possessed already a deep knowledge of birds, but also loved them with a passionate appreciation of their beauty. It was even more odd in William, since he had learned so soon to loathe the idea of death and of the slaughter of farm animals. But it would be inapt to lay any great stress on this inconsistency. The act of shooting—of simply firing a gun and seeing a distant bird fall—was too impersonal to seem like killing, compared with a butcher's use of the knife. Again, although Daniel Hudson himself did not care to shoot, a cold roast duck was his favourite breakfast dish, and this, with other game, the boys would as a matter of course provide. William, too, had the normal instincts of any boy, anxious to copy his elders and show off his own skill, without allowing imagination to spoil his sport.

In that country, indeed, childhood was short, as they were reminded when the war snatched away their fifteen-year-old playmate Dardo into the native army. Dardo was one of a band of lads, sons of shepherds or gauchos, with whom William and Albert played. The two elder Hudson boys had by this time outgrown rough-and-tumble sports such as mock battles on horseback, using green poplar boughs as lances; or "hunting the ostrich", when William, fastest and most dexterous, would be chosen as "ostrich", to run and jump and dodge the pursuing "hunters" until brought down by the *bolas* (a light imitation of the weighted lasso with which the real bird was caught), and "cut up" by the hunters. Pony races were another diversion, and at race meetings in the neighbourhood their father would give them money to enter the boys' events; but, even when their ponies were superior, the cunning native lads could usually play some trick to prevent their winning.

When William was born, on St. Dominic's day, Spanish neighbours begged his mother to call him after his natal saint, and were bitterly disappointed at her refusal. To themselves, however, he was always known as Dominic, and this name may well have suited better the eager, dark-eyed, brown-skinned boy, who was so lively and aloof by turns.

The neighbours, for their part, with their vivid looks and bizarre personalities, fascinated the child. The young bird-watcher, himself shy as a wild bird with strangers, loitering on his pony about the trees of their homesteads, often miles from his own home, had been a familiar sight in the district since William was six or seven years old; and in time he was persuaded to talk to the people he met.

These clumps of ancient trees had been planted by early colonists then still following the Spanish rural way of life. The trees surrounded low reed-thatched houses, built of brick or of clay and brushwood. There would be no gardens, except sometimes a few flowers and a patch of herbs, parsley, rue, sage, tansy and horehound, to be used either in flavouring the unvarying diet of meat, or as simple remedies in illness. It was little wonder if curiosity were aroused in the ranchers by newcomers like "Don Daniel", taking such pride in the size and flavour of his potatoes; or his wife, buying coffee from the city to give to her household instead of maté for breakfast, and pickling great casks of peaches in vinegar, and making enough peach jam to last the year round, instead of turning her family loose in the orchard, like a litter of little pigs, as long as the ripe crop lasted; or the youngsters themselves, accustomed to eat vegetables, salads, fruit pies and maize-meal bread as happily as their own children might take a bone of cold meat.

One old woman, living in a poplar-shaded house by a bird-haunted stream which William loved, would waylay him whenever she could in order to question him about these odd customs. White-haired, with laughing eyes and wrinkled brown face, and perpetually smoking a cigar, she possessed also a remarkably dictatorial nature. William remembered her coming in triumph, after a long spell of rain which had threatened the district with floods, to assure his mother that she had settled matters by hanging an image of St. Anthony (her patron saint) in the well, by way of an object-lesson.

Another sorry-looking house, without garden or trees, was nevertheless the home of an important landowner, Don Evaristo Peñalva, a descendant of one of the aristocratic Spanish families who had settled in the country in the seventeenth and eighteenth centuries. This dignified old patriarch, with his six wives and swarming family, was the learned man or wizard of that part. Among his accomplishments was a cure for shingles (a common and serious malady) by a happy blend of Christian and pagan lore—writing on the patient's skin, in pen and ink, the benediction beginning *In the name of the Father*, and then simply rubbing him with a toad.

Another character, Don Anastacio, managed to combine the vocation of exquisite with that of pig-fancier. A yeasty Osric of the plains, he arranged his hair in ringlets, wore the embroidered blouse, yellow kilt, lace drawers and scarlet-lined cloak of the gaucho costume, and passed his time agreeably in sipping maté and admiring his herd of wild red pigs.

A horse-breeder, Don Gregorio Gandara, was chiefly remarkable for his vast herds of piebalds, which, with their varied colourings, were striking and beautiful. To the Hudson children, however, his house had an attraction quite apart from his horses. This was a pet ostrich which loved human company, but could not be allowed in the house owing to its taste for swallowing scissors, spoons, thimbles and any other treasures it could find. It would follow the young ones happily when they escaped into the orchard, and they liked to give it half a dozen peaches at once, and then watch the absurd sequence of round lumps proceeding slowly down the long neck.

More congenial to their parents was the company of the nearest English neighbour, Mr. Royd, with his alert mind, fun-loving, happy disposition, and his

c

unfailing enthusiasms and projects. These ranged from
the building of a fantastic wooden carriage for his
family, to an attempt to make a fortune from sheep's-
milk cheeses.

Chance visitors were made welcome by the Hudsons,
although if the guest were eccentric or uncouth this
could prove a trial: their kind-hearted mother trying
to put the newcomer at his ease, the father casting
glances of stern warning at the children, while they sat
entranced, drinking in the visitor's oddities in order to
imitate them afterwards. For a different reason, however, William remembered one of these travellers. He
was a graceful young Spaniard, who at first charmed
them all by playing his guitar as they sat in the fire-
light; then, laying it down, told the parents that he
could play no longer, as their fireside reminded him
too poignantly of his own far-off home, and of evenings
spent in reading, talking and singing with his brothers
and sisters—a tribute which Caroline Hudson liked
afterward to recall.

But the harmony and security of this family life, in
which a natural habit of reserve left each child free to
follow his own path, were already threatened by the
downward curve of Daniel Hudson's fortunes. It was
true, as he and his wife must have surmised in coming
to the Argentine, that this was a prosperous land, where
sheep and cattle-breeding and trading were money-
making pursuits. Yet the same native cunning which
allowed the gaucho boys to beat the young Hudsons
at racing, despite their inferior ponies, outwitted the
father in his business dealings; and he was too trustful
and too innately honest to learn from his mistakes.

State archives show that the land he bought in 1837
was still intact in his possession two years later. In

1841, the year of William's birth, he apparently sold two pieces of land, each about 500 varas (rather less than a third of a mile) in width. He now owned, in partnership, three hundred head of cattle and two hundred and fifty sheep, together with the portion of land remaining, which would not be enough to maintain the stock; so that, unless he owned grazing rights, further land must have been hired.

In 1846, when they decided to move, "The Twenty-five Ombús" was left in the care of servants. These may have acted as caretakers only, if the land were let to someone else; or, if Daniel Hudson kept his share in the partnership, as stockmen also.

Ezequiel Martinez Estrada records that these servants had the famous tiles stripped from the roof, and replaced them with thatch; most native houses on the pampas being roofed with sedge or bulrushes.

The kind of country store which Daniel took over at "The Acacias" might, in other hands, have been as profitable as were cattle and sheep—in other hands; but it is clear that, when misfortune overtook the family in William's sixteenth year, there was little money left for a fresh start, or to pay for more labour than the three sons then at home could give.

But on William, at fourteen, the shadow of these anxieties had not yet fallen. With a younger brother as his companion, or alone with his private enchantments, he was happy. If ever he thought of the future, he did so perhaps with a little dread, as a time when the beautiful years of his life would be over and he must turn like other men to some practical career.

He prayed meanwhile that time might stand still, while he lay on the grass, watching the flight of thistle-down or the movements of a bird making its nest.

Chapter II

Studies: For Life and Death

Buenos Aires, with its crowded streets and markets, so fascinating to him after the quieter life of the estancia, was also in those days a place of pestilence, without water or drainage systems. Drinking water was sold in muddy buckets by watermen, or taken, alive with mosquito larvae, from rainwater cisterns. The city was flanked by atrocious killing-grounds where herds of beeves were slaughtered daily under the hot sun. Here, bones, flesh and offal in heaps were left to the carrion-hawks; blood and dust mingled to form a thick crust over the whole area; and thousands of skulls were used, as are loose stones in hill country, as a macabre kind of fencing for orchards.

The city was soon to become notorious, from deadly outbreaks of typhus, cholera and yellow fever, as the most unhealthy in the world. On a long holiday there, William was soon conscious of a strange sense of lassitude, even while he eagerly explored the streets and bird-markets, or as he sat fishing by the river front. This he attributed to the change from riding to walking, and from turf to hard pavements. But soon after his return home he collapsed with typhoid. In that isolated spot, far from medical help, the fever would have killed him but for his mother's skill. The attack left him thin as a skeleton, unable to stand or speak. Slowly, after months of weakness, the invalid recovered sufficiently to sit in the spring sunlight, enjoying the scent of earth and songs of birds, and the company of his brothers and sisters.

On his fifteenth birthday, still filled with wonder at finding that he was alive, he suddenly asked himself, *What do I want? What do I ask to have?*—crying in spirit, with the ardent voice of the young Shelley, *O World, O Life, O Time!*

The answer was startlingly clear, but it was one which he dared not yet accept. "I want only to keep what I have; to rise each morning and look out on the sky and the grassy dew-wet earth from day to day, from year to year. To watch each June and July for spring, to feel the same old sweet surprise and delight at the appearance of each familiar flower, every new-born insect, every bird returned once more from the north. To listen in a trance of delight to the wild notes of the golden plover coming once more to the great plain, flying, flying south, flock succeeding flock the whole day long. . . ."

William understood at last that this answer was the right one; yet while he was unable any longer to shun the thought of the future, he was unable also to see any link between the desire for freedom and for the "earth life" he loved, and the necessity for men to earn their bread. Even when the link was forged, indeed, it remained until near the end of his life most pitifully tenuous, so that forty years later he was writing defiantly: "Better, I say, to live as I do on rather less than £100 a year and be free—yes, free even from life's 'pleasures'." Still later, in a mood of reaction, he spoke enviously of the happy life of a heath-cutter beside that of himself, scarcely more remunerative, as a writer.

It is not everyone who, looking back in later life, can feel that he would win the approval of his fifteen-year-old self. Conversely, to poor young William, so anxiously reproaching himself for idleness and lack of ambition, the success and honours of his old age— represented in the ability to earn that modest and elusive hundred pounds a year in observing and describing wild life—would have seemed unbelievable felicity.

At this point, he lacked confidence to assure himself that it was right for him to shape his future in his own way. He saw that Daniel and Edwin had at his age put away childish things, giving up outdoor games and pastimes for "the dull business of life", the one on the ranch, the other in study. These paths were closed to him, as he had neither Daniel's strength nor Edwin's aptitude; but, while conscience spurred him into making a resolution, instinct led him to choose a right course. In a spirit of compromise, he decided to continue his bird-watching and rides about the plain, but to start also on a course of serious reading.

Up to this time he had read little, and written not at all. Inspired by a painting he had seen, depicting the kind of pampas landscape he knew so well, he thought for a time of becoming a painter; and, although this idea did not prosper, he was to keep always some interest in drawing, a fondness for the company of painters, and a fondness too for illustrating his letters to friends with little sketches, usually of birds. But, as his schoolmasters found, no indoor occupation could compare for him in fascination with the outdoor world. As a child he had, however, enjoyed a few of the story-books which began to appear early in the nine-teenth century: "The Discontented Squirrel" was one little fable read and re-read at seven years old, because the squirrel, like himself, longed to follow the birds in their migration southward—a theme of life-long interest to him. Among three or four hundred volumes on the family bookshelves he had discovered a few others which appealed to him for similar reasons. Chief among these was a Natural History and two small books about birds. There was also an eighteenth-century Geography from which he had filched a print of Stonehenge (which he imagined standing, high as the heavens, on a plain vast as his own pampas). He had discovered, too, that poets, like the landscape painter, and unlike the more scientific writers, seemed to share his own delight in nature; and that a few lines of pastoral poetry would give him more pleasure, and accorded better with his feelings, than a whole book in prose on the same subject. The only volume of verse on the shelves was a collection by Shenstone, and the boy's natural intelligence soon rejected the banalities of his "bright Roxana tripping o'er the green" and similar themes. He was obliged to content himself, however, with the few passages of higher quality (though still the work only of minor poets) quoted in prose works.

A favourite was one by an obscure Sussex writer, the Rev. James Hurdis, whose sentiments William could appreciate when, for instance, he philosophised on the skill of a nesting bird:

> It was my admiration
> To view the structure of that little work,
> A bird's nest—mark it well, within, without;
> No tool had he that wrought, no knife to cut,
> No rail to fix, no bodkin to insert,
> No glue to join: his little beak was all:

And yet how neatly finished! What nice hand,
With every implement and means of art,
And twenty years' apprenticeship to boot,
Could make me such another? Fondly then
We boast of excellence, whose noblest skill
Instinctive genius foils!

One day, on another visit to Buenos Aires, he had
unearthed from among masses of Spanish, French and
German books in a dusty secondhand bookshop, a
copy of Thomson's *Seasons*. This—the first book he
had ever bought for himself—seemed a lavish feast
after those crumbs of verse found in the dull tomes of
theology, history, science or philosophy at home. Keats
in discovering Chapman's *Homer* can have felt no keener
happiness than young William, drinking in Thomson's
warm and vigorous idiom in page after page of loving
description; for example, the "mingled wilderness of
flowers", with

> The yellow wall-flower, stained with iron brown,
> And lavish stock, that scents the garden round:
> From the soft wing of vernal breezes shed,
> Anemones, auriculas, enriched
> With shining meal o'er all their velvet leaves. . . .

Such old-world flowers could be found growing half-
wild about many farmhouses on the plain. Even more
eagerly he would read the long passages about English
birds, such as the naïve and charming account of the
robin, that in winter

> Wisely regardful of the embroiling sky,
> In joyless fields and thorny thickets leaves
> His shivering mates, and pays to trusted man
> His annual visit. . . .

40

Encouraged by this happy find, William had returned to the shop, and there discovered another pastoral poem—Robert Bloomfield's *Farmer's Boy*, joyfully recognised as the source of certain quotations already learned by heart. This simple work, written by a Suffolk countryman while living in a London garret, had had a remarkable vogue after its publication in 1800. It was a long quiet abstract of the rural scene from season to season, in the tradition of Spencer, Cowper and Thomson himself. Its value to William lay in the fact that he felt himself presented at last, not with tantalising fragments and snippets, but with a sober, lengthy, detailed account of the English countryside, and its way of life—England, which had for him already become his spiritual home, "the land of my desire".

These scanty treasures evoked in William a lasting loyalty and gratitude to minor poets, which survived after years of reading at the British Museum library, where he became familiar with classics denied to him as a boy. On his death-bed, as though his debt to Hurdis, Thomson and Bloomfield were not yet discharged, he was still testifying to this interest in a last unfinished fragment of writing.

Meanwhile the boy's love of books was growing as was his love of nature, and this too was to last all his life. He read and grew fond of *Tristram Shandy*, Spanish romances, and Chesterfield's *Letters*, which he found in an old eighteenth-century edition; but he was also venturing on more serious works, such as Rollin's *Ancient History* (a name familiar to readers of early American books for children). Its two great quarto volumes, lavishly illustrated, provided another stimulus to his awakening intellect. Many boys of fifteen would have found it a prosaic task, but, to William, Rollin proved as fascinating as Edwin's nightly stories in the old days; and the youngster went on eagerly to a *History of Christianity* in eighteen volumes, then to a study of ancient mythologies and philosophies, and next took a long leap forward to Carlyle's *French Revolution*.

Such reading, although it helped to satisfy his new appetite for study, did little to solve the question of a niche in life; but now came an event momentous in his career. A discerning old family friend, who took an interest in him and his bird-watching, brought him from London a copy of Gilbert White's *Natural History of Selborne*.

In all his fifteen years—as in the fifteen years that followed—surrounded as he was by some of the most beautiful and striking birds, animals, flowers, snakes and insects to be found in any part of the earth, William had never met another soul with whom he could speak of his love for them. To his mother he might have done so, as he later realised, but she had little leisure to cultivate her children's minds through intimate discussions. His little sister, Mary Ellen, had a great fondness for animals, and would befriend forlorn creatures: once, to the family's amusement, she had made a pet of a motherless lamb, on which she lavished affection, washing its fleece every day with scented soap, and hanging garlands of scarlet verbenas about its neck. But such charming fancy could not match William's fervent animism. There was no one who, by sharing his feelings, could give him confidence in their value, and defend him against the charge of slothfulness. Like the young Richard Jefferies, he was painfully aware (as the sensitive exceptional youth must often be aware) of this neighbourly criticism of his "idleness"—criticism the more wounding for its lack of understanding.

This volume, forged in the lanes and hanging beech-woods of far-away Hampshire, came to him as a sunlit revelation. In Gilbert White he found himself for the first time in touch with a kindred mind. One may well imagine his sympathetic pleasure in such passages as: "The most unusual birds I ever observed in these parts were a pair of hoopoes (*upupa*), which came several years ago in the summer, and frequented an ornamental piece of ground, which joins to my garden, for some weeks. They used to march about in a stately manner, feeding in the walks, many times in the day; and seemed disposed to breed in my outlet; but were frightened and persecuted by idle boys, who would never let them be at rest." (Letter XI.)

"It pleases me to find that my account of the *ousel migration* pleases you. You put a very shrewd question when you ask me how I know that their autumnal migration is southward? Were not candour and openness the very life of natural history, I should pass over this query just as a sly commentator does over a crabbed passage in a classic; but common ingenuousness obliges me to confess, not without some degree of shame, that I only reasoned in that case from analogy. For as all other autumnal birds migrate from the north-word to us, to partake of our milder winters, and return to the northward again when the rigorous cold abates, so I concluded that the ring-ousels did the same." (Letter XXVI.)

Here was the impetus he sought, and the warranty of his profession, signed by the "father of field naturalists" himself. Whether or not he realised this at once, *Selborne*, like a fingerpost, pointed him forward, and he started out lighthearted from this friendship and inspiration. He began to keep a diary, recording the sights and sounds and the weather of each day, in faithful imitation. The surrounding plain, with its marshes and thistle-fields, streams and plantations, became in secret "my parish of Selborne"; and he studied the pages until, like Mary Russell Mitford, he knew them by heart and could "form a friendship with the fields and coppices, as well as with the birds, mice and squirrels who inhabit them".

The letters of the Selborne curate to Thomas Pennant, Esq., and to the Hon. Daines Barrington had another important outcome; for one cannot doubt that they were the model on which was formed William's own initial work, the foundation of his career as a writer—his letters to the Zoological Society of London.

These, however, were not yet to appear. They would mark the climax of his long apprenticeship. But he was not to follow even this difficult path without cruel hindrance. Continuing his studies, he was deep in Gibbon's *Decline and Fall of the Roman Empire* when another blow fell, this time involving the whole family.

It appeared that Daniel Hudson, in taking over the derelict ranch and homestead of "The Acacias", ten years before, had neglected to safeguard his property by deed. The place, restored from decay by his efforts and capital, should have become a permanent family home and provided a living for his sons; but now a counter-claim was made and legally upheld. Possibly this arose from new land legislation in about this period. Whatever the reason, the outcome was that the property passed into other hands, and the unfortunate

Hudsons were obliged to go back to live, in poverty, at their one remaining possession, "The Twenty-five Ombús".

Here Daniel again started a small store or inn, which became known in the countryside as "Uson's" or Don Daniel's store. His son the younger Daniel, with William and Albert, worked on the ranch, attended to the livestock and helped in various trading enterprises. Records show that in 1858 the father hired extra workmen to help in moving a load of eighty kilos of horsehair and two hundred and forty sheep-skins—a small undertaking for a regular dealer, yet a large one for a cattle-farmer: it seems likely, therefore, that for the remaining years of his life Daniel drifted between the two occupations of shopkeeper and rancher. By 1862 (when a register office for title-deeds was created by law) his capital was less than £1,000, while the census of 1865 shows that the land at the "Twenty-five Ombús" had been reduced to a quarter of its original extent.

William, endowed with the two-fold stoicism of the field naturalist and the happy "poor scholar", did not feel the change of fortune deeply; but soon he himself fell victim to a second disaster which threatened to end all his hopes, and even life itself. He had grown fast, becoming tall and thin, and his earlier illness may have left him more delicate than anyone suspected; but his sensitive need to justify private studies by practical work led him into efforts beyond his strength. One winter day, driving a herd of cattle home from a distant ranch, he was exposed for many hours to wind and rain, and became soaked, exhausted and numb with cold as he struggled with the restive herd. An attack of rheumatic fever followed, which so severely affected

45

his heart that doctors in Buenos Aires declared that his case was hopeless, and that he might drop dead at any moment.

That dreadful pronouncement threw over his next years, the years of learning and young manhood, in which his gifts and ideas would have had time to flower, a shadow so deep that afterward he could scarcely bear to recall them. His early dread of death, returning in full force, plunged him into a search for religious truth in the sombre volumes of theology and sermons on the familiar bookshelves. These, formerly glanced through hastily in the light-hearted quest for snatches of poetry, became at this dark time the scene of his struggle for the one thing that now mattered to him supremely—the hope of life after death. In his agony of mind, the boy compared himself to the tortured prisoners of Argentine soldiers, bound and helpless, waiting for death while their captors taunted them with the knife. It seemed to him that the sufferings of the damned, described at length in such works as Baxter's *Saints' Everlasting Rest*, and to which he seemed condemned from his want of faith, would be more bearable than total annihilation— a nadir of distress shared by many others at this period, during what one writer has termed "the process of robbing millions of pious souls of their hope of eternal damnation". For William, at least, this distress was genuine and deserved more sympathy than such a comment implies. Sometimes, after weeks of prayer and mental conflict, he would have an interval of peace, when he believed that he had found reassurance; then doubts would return, as he remembered some tale or read some fresh passage which seemed to dismiss his belief in survival as a delusion.

He was conscious that his mother, supported through-out her own hard life by her faith, watched his struggle with anxiety, although the habit of reticence prevented her speaking of it openly. Of his physical sufferings in these sad years he could at least tell her; but he was soon to lose her sympathy and care, with all that it meant to him, and the love which he felt as "a prescience of immortality". Two months after his eighteenth birthday, on October 4th, 1859, she died after a brief illness. Her last words to William were of her distress at leaving him to contend alone with his broken health and troubled spirit.

Edwin, returning home after five years' absence, had become a learned and well-mannered young man of the world, of whom the younger brother now found himself somewhat in awe. He added to William's problems by giving him Darwin's *Origin of Species*. It is perhaps difficult, in looking back a hundred years, to appreciate the mighty storm which the doctrine of evolution raised, throughout the world, in Christians who had never consciously doubted the truth of Biblical teaching; but one can imagine the corresponding up-heaval in the mind of this youth, who, though knowing little of debates in the outer world, was trying under sentence of death to find a creed for himself. Rejecting Darwin's theory at first with hostility, he was wisely advised by Edwin to read the book again, not as an orthodox believer but as a naturalist. By degrees he accepted the theory as an incontrovertible truth, and he even began to wonder, as a naturalist, that it should never before have been formulated.

How closely his physical and mental anguish were linked, however, became clear when at last, with in-tervals of freedom from heart trouble, the doubts and

47

fears torturing his mind began also to fade. For a long time still he was to suffer agonising heart attacks, and at twenty, having strained his eyes, he was threatened for a time with blindness and forced to give up his books. Then, finding through desperate experiment that riding and walking made the heart attacks no worse, he slowly resumed his old habits. From a brave resolve to see as much more of his native land as he could before death should overtake him, he began the adventurous wandering life which he was to lead for the next fifteen years.

CHAPTER III

The Bird-Collector

THE FIVE sons and daughters who had made up
the household since Edwin's departure were still
living with their father at "The Twenty-five
Ombús"; but from this time onwards William was
often away, staying with friends in the city or in distant
homes on the plain; and at other times riding, as he
had done from childhood, about the countryside. Like
his hero of *The Purple Land*, he would pass from homestead to homestead, charming their life-histories from
lonely men and women starving for a new listener;
or following the gaucho way of life for which his
Spanish looks and his love of freedom, if not his
physique, fitted him. Then he would work by day
with cattle, and at night join the circle about the
camp-fire to hear his companions' songs and stories.
As country people in other parts of the world help one
another at harvest, so the young cowboys would share
in the yearly 'parting' and branding of the half-grown
cattle that roamed almost wild on the plains: and each
dangerous and exciting day's work, calling for the
greatest skill as horseman and with the lasso, would
be followed by evening dances and merrymaking.

Typical of his life in these years was an account he
gave long afterwards, of a visit to a ranch belonging
to one of his brothers, in a part of the country still
exposed to Indian raids.

"I only went once to stay with him," he told his

friend Morley Roberts, "and I rode there with no more than two horses, and they got pretty tired too, and one night, a good time after sunset, I heard galloping, and two Indians charged down on me. At least, I thought they meant to knock me over and take the horses, but I pulled up and got my revolver out, and they, finding me wide awake, swerved and passed me galloping. One of them as he rode past squealed in the curious, high-pitched voice the Indians always use in talking Spanish, 'Friend, your horses are tired!' They passed me like a whirlwind, and very late I got to my brother's. I didn't stay there long, it was far too much exposed to incursions from the south. As a matter of fact I didn't sleep there. My brother and I used to go together to another house not far off and stay the night. There were more men there. A lot of us galloped together. We used to tell stories, sitting and smoking, but there was no one in any way pre-eminent, until one evening a very poorly clad gaucho came in.

"He had only one horse, and as usual begged permission to stay there that night and make his bed. So when his horse was turned loose he brought in his saddle and presently, after answering all the usual questions and asking such as occurred to him, he began to talk and attracted everybody's attention. The man was a strange and wonderful genius. He talked about everything: the country and its condition, politics and statesmen, the condition of the poor man, the follies and wickedness of the rich, but all in such a high strain of true, natural eloquence that he kept us on the stretch to hear every word he said. After he poured forth what seemed like untold riches hour after hour he stopped talking and rolled a cigarette, and then one or the other of us asked him some question and set him going again, so that it was almost dawn before we were satisfied and went to sleep. So far as words were concerned he was the greatest genius I ever saw. . . ."

Riding about the province to its southern and western frontiers, filling his notebooks with descriptions and strange tales of wild life and human beings, Hudson's ambitions for a time narrowed and hardened. From the early love of looking at and living in nature with the sensuous delight of the poet, there grew the desire to become a professional naturalist and observer, and to win recognition as an authority on the birds of his country—an ambition which was to meet with no little success. That first training in recording facts, begun under the stimulus of reading Gilbert White and the keeping of his naturalist's diary, now continued alongside an acquisitive career as a bird-collector, which was, nevertheless, also of the greatest educative value to the budding writer on nature.

He was twenty-four years old when, on December 27th, 1865, Hinton Rowan Helper, United States consul in Buenos Aires, wrote on his behalf to Dr. Spencer Fullerton Baird, assistant secretary of the renowned Smithsonian Institution in Washington. Dr. Baird was occupied at that time in supervising explorations in North and South America. Mr. Helper's letter explained that Professor German Burmeister (director of the natural history museum in Buenos Aires) had introduced to the writer "a Mr. Wm. H. Hudson, of Conchitas, Partido de Quilmes, in this Republic—a sort of amateur ornithologist, who would like to be employed in collecting birds. . . . Mr. Hudson has been recommended to me as quite capable in what he professes. I have asked him for his terms; but he says he has never made any collections except as a matter of mere interest to himself; and does not, therefore, know how to charge for his services". The consul suggested, in view of this diffidence, that Mr. Hudson should be paid "so much for such and such birds".

Dr. Baird, in his reply two months later, observed that he could not find Conchitas on any map, but that little was known of the birds in the Republic, and it would therefore give him much pleasure to see Mr. Hudson's collections and help him in disposing of them. Small, inconspicuous birds, he added, were of the greatest scientific interest; and various prices were suggested.

Six months later, on September 5th, 1866, Hudson sat down at "The Twenty-five Ombús" and carefully copied, on a page cut from his notebook, the letter he had composed to Dr. Baird. This (except for a few lines quoted from his diary and written on March 18th, 1865) is the earliest of his writings to survive to the present day:

Dear Sir,

Mr. Helper kindly favored me with a copy of your letter to him, in reference to my collecting birds. I hoped then, to have had, before September, two or three hundred specimans, but I have been disappointed: winter birds, which I tried to collect, were so very scarce this season, that several times I have ridden leagues without being able to obtain, or even see, a single speciman. Most of the birds I now send are those that remain with us all the year, and are all probably well known to naturalists: it is too early yet for summer birds, and as I will not collect any more for two or three weeks I think it best to send the few I have got.

I am not confident that they will reach you in a good state of preservation, as I have no experience in this kind of work; however, they are not many to lose, if they should be lost, and by the time your answer reaches me, I hope to have many more ready to send. I will also try to obtain some ostrich eggs, and a box of snail shells, of which I believe there are only four species in this country.

As you have not required the names of the birds, I have only thought it nessisary to mark the sex of each one, on the margin of the paper in which it is wraped; but if you desire it, in future, I can give, with each species, a concise account of its habits. As to the locality in which they were killed, I shot them all within eight leagues of Buenos Ayres City.

You remark that the birds best to get are the small inconspicuous ones, as they are better for scientific purposes. By diligently searching through the swampy forrests along the river, I can obtain many birds of this description. There are here many species of the *certhia* an extensive genus of small and homely birds. And it is reasonable to expect, that in a country so little explored by naturalists as this, many species may be found unknown to science.

You must know from the physical conditions of this country—the Province of Buenos Ayres—that it possesses a very scanty Fauna. Wide as is its extent, it is but one vast, level and almost treeless plain, affording no shelter to bird or beast from the cold South winds of winter or the scorching North winds that blow incessantly in summer: while the yearly droughts banish all the aquatic birds to great distances. But it is not only that there are few species, that makes the work of a mere taxadermist unprofitable but these are often so widly seperated that vast tracts must be traversed to obtain them all. Though I am not a person of means, it is not from want of other employment I desire to collect, but purly from a love of nature. It would, however, be eisier for me to devote all my time to these pursuits, if I was required to collect other natural objects besides birds, as fossils, insects, grasses, etc. and this would enable me to make thorough collections of all the birds. I am, Sir,

Respectfully yours,

WILLIAM H. HUDSON.

One may imagine with what professional pride Hudson would have seen recorded in the Institution's Report for 1866: "In South America, explorations have been made and collections transmitted by Mr. W. H. Hudson, in Buenos Ayres." Some of the bird-skins which he prepared and sent are still to be seen in the Institution's collections at Washington. An observer has pointed out that these are easily distinguished, as, unversed in formal taxidermy, Hudson had folded the legs forward instead of backward.

During the year 1866 another duty intervened. Having already done his military service according to law, he was again recruited (as "Soldier No. 22") when the National Guard was called out over the whole Argentine territory on the outbreak of war with Paraguay, and was sent with his brother Daniel to the frontier, to the Guardia del Azul, where he served for several months.

Now followed the peak year of his career as a collector. No less than 123 bird-skins were dispatched to Dr. Baird, duplicates being also prepared for his own private collection. The Institution's Report for 1867 paid tribute to this success, noting that "an important Smithsonian exploration has been made in the Province of Buenos Ayres by Mr. W. H. Hudson, who has transmitted large collections of birds, which have been referred to Mr. P. L. Sclater and Mr. Osbert Salvin, of London, for examination, these gentlemen having been especially occupied in the study of South American birds".

Of 163 collections recorded as having been sent to the Institution in that year, Hudson's was given special mention as among the eight most important. Fourteen of the species sent were not on Professor

Burmeister's list—the most complete at the time for that region.

It was Hudson's dream to discover a new species —"some bird", as he later wrote, "as beautiful as the wryneck or wheatear, and as old on earth, but which had never been named and never even seen by any appreciative human eye". In June 1867, when dispatching one of these boxes of skins, he wrote to Dr. Baird drawing his attention to some "blackbirds" which he believed might fulfil this hope. But this time he was disappointed: the bird was *Molothrus rufoaxillaris*, and had been recorded and named as such by an American ornithologist only a few months before. It was Patagonia, that strange and legendary land which already called to him with promises of new wonders, which was to grant him this wish and add the name *enipolegus hudsoni*, or Hudson's tyrant-bird, to the lists of science.

Still unaware that he was to be disappointed, he wrote again to Dr. Baird in March 1868, diplomatically observing that "Dr. Burmeister would like to know" what name was to be given to the blackbird. With this letter he apparently enclosed a photograph of himself, taken at the studio of "Meeks y Kelsey, fotografos, 74, Belgano, Buenos Ayres"; and this, together with his letters, was to lie undiscovered in the files at Washington for nearly eighty years.

But already his need for fresh worlds was becoming imperative; by June 1867 he was writing, "It is impossible for me to make complete collections while I remain at home." His last strong link with "The Twenty-five Ombús" was about to be broken. On January 14th, 1868, at the age of sixty-four, his father died. Fond as he was of his brothers and sisters,

Hudson felt his time in that part of the world was now drawing to its close.

His personal grief was mingled with the wretchedness he felt in his country's sufferings during the prolonged war with Paraguay. A few weeks after his father's death he was writing to Dr. Baird, advising him to address letters to Buenos Aires city, as war had greatly disorganised the mails, and adding: "For several months I have not collected any birds at all, as I have had other occupations at home, besides we have not been exempt from the afflictions that have come on almost every household in this country."

A few months later, on June 3rd, he wrote: "At present I am so occupied with other matters that I do not collect, but still cherish the hope that I will soon be able to give my whole time to a pursuit that affords me so much pleasure: I will, of course, leave the Conchitas, as I think you will not require more duplicates of the species to be obtained here." The last mention of Hudson's name in the Institution's reports came in 1869 with the entry: "Hudson, W. H. Two boxes birds, Buenos Ayres."

Meanwhile, another chapter had opened in his life. Sclater and Salvin, the two London ornithologists to whom his collections had been sent, gave an account of their studies at a session of the Zoological Society in February 1868; and Dr. Sclater himself wrote to tell Hudson that a report of this account would be published in the Society's *Proceedings*, and that a copy would be sent to him.

Thus another milestone was passed, Hudson's name appearing for the first time in an English publication. The article was headed, "List of Birds Collected at

Conchitas, Argentine Republic, by Mr. William H. Hudson", and contained the encouraging invitation, "We trust that Mr. Hudson will continue his collections in this interesting locality, and that we may again have the pleasure of calling the Society's attention to this subject."

The promised copy sent to him did not arrive, and a year later, on April 30th, 1869, he wrote to Dr. Sclater from a friend's house in Buenos Aires: "I owe you an apology for allowing your letter tc remain so long unanswered, I did not write when it was recieved hoping first to see the copy of the report refered to in your letter. The copy you sent never reached me, and as I have been much of the time absent from home my answer was delayed till now.

"One copy of the report sent to Dr. Burmeister has just reached me, and I have looked over it with much pleasure. I regret to find that I have made so great a mistake as to mark females two of the tree black plumaged Silver-bills. . . . This was pure carelessness as all the black plumaged birds I have ever opened were males, the red, females. I have also watched them pairing and building their nest, and am therefore quite positive they are sexes, though country people here regard them as different species. There is also another mistake of less importance, the vulgar name of the Scolqux frenata is *patas amarillas* (yellow feet) the Becasina is another bird. . . .

"It depends upon Dr. Baird's answer to my last letter wethear I shall continue to collect for him or not. There are not many more birds to be obtained in this district, and the price I am paid (90 cents a speciman) would not pay my expenses, should I extend my researches a distance from home."

Evidently Dr. Baird's awaited answer was unfavourable, since after the 1869 entry his name disappeared from the Smithsonian reports, although he did not lose touch altogether with the Institution. In the next two years, however, his link with the London Zoological Society strengthened, and his niche as a collector seemed assured, even though this was clearly a scanty living. Two further reports of his collections appeared in the *Proceedings*: the third (published in 1869) showing that these had totalled 143 species, many of which were almost unknown to European ornithologists. In September of that year he took another step forward in venturing to write to Dr. Sclater with the modest suggestion:

"I have from time to time made notes on the habits of the birds, etc., of the Pampas and would like much to know if they would be of any importance to naturalists, perhaps you will kindly favor me with your opinions on this subject."

Dr. Sclater's reply, welcoming this tentative offer, marked the beginning of a correspondence which he edited and published in the Society's *Proceedings* during 1870 and 1871. Thus Hudson's first published work resembled White's *Selborne* in being composed of essays written in letter form: and among the virtues which the young writer happily imitated was that directness and simplicity of approach, the fervent absorption and pleasure in his own information, which marks the Selborne letters. Again, although he had not taken pains to observe the spelling (for instance) of the word "specimen" from his master, Hudson had learned something far more important both to himself and his readers—to despise any hint of distortion of facts for the sake of a favourite theory. In that admission of "pure carelessness", which must have appeared with a certain boyish air in the austere pages of the *Proceedings*, may be heard the echo of the eighteenth-century naturalist telling Thomas Pennant Esq.; "Notwithstanding what I have said in a former letter, no grey crows were ever known to breed on Dartmoor; it was my mistake."

The first letter, written on December 14th, 1869, shows vividly how, even at this early stage, with his uncertain command of language, his sentences could melt into music when he began to speak of birds. He opened his letter with a description of the floating islands of the *camaloté*, the water-lily of the Paraña and its tributaries, which, sweeping down the great rivers, brought new species of seeds, animals, snakes and toads from the north to the swampy thickets bordering the Plata; the "grand highway" by which, as he believed, new species of birds also arrived in the region. As the essay continues, brief glimpses of Hudson's life as a bird-watcher are revealed, as when, for example, he describes a species of cuckoo:

"Like the common cuckoo it is retiring in its habits, concealing itself in the densest foliage, but it cannot be attracted like the other species, by mimicking its call.

"It has a song, which it will sometimes repeat at short intervals for half a day, it is like the mourning of our little dove, being a succession of long and plaintive notes . . . so much resembling the cry of another bird that I was frequently decieved by it. . . .

"I frequently spent half a day watching for and pursuing them. Once only I succeeded in getting a glimpse of one, at the moment it started screaming from a tree. I was, fortunately, able to secure it, and have it still in my collection. . . ."

Further on appears this poignant description, which for all the cool detachment of the telling, can scarcely have failed to touch the feelings even of this keen collector.

"Another bird of very interesting habits and never seen away from the river wood is the *Icterus pyrrhopterus* . . . it has a continuos song, sweet, low and varied, with a peculiar ventriloquism in some notes, that give the listener a confused idea that the performer approaches and retires while singing. The first bird of this species I shot, was but slightly wounded in the wing, and fell into a stream; to my great surprise it began singing as it floated about on the surface of the water, and even when I had taken it out, continued to sing at intervals in my hand. . . .

"In a few days I returned to the spot to secure the nest and observe them again, but found to my sorrow nest and birds had disappeared."

His sorrow, quite clearly, was not for the destruction of the nest, nor for the distress of the parent birds, which he had observed with professional detachment—"the male and female fluttered round me manafesting great anxiety"—but for his own loss of a valuable specimen. This attitude, and the whole tone of the passage, might have seemed incredible to those who in later life were to know him as the ardent protector of birds, and to know, too, his prejudice against science in its cold and heartless aspects.

Yet, to his closer friends, this would not be so. Just as in boyhood he had worshipped bird life and also enjoyed shooting, so to the end of his days he retained a certain callous interest in suffering as an inevitable part of life, and therefore acceptable. He once remarked that he had experimented by allowing bees and wasps to sting him "for the experience". Moreover, he always realised that bird-skins were necessary to the study of ornithology: it was the stuffed bird, "something pretty in a glass case", the "feathered woman" and the "linnet for sixpence" which aroused his anger. Certainly there was no sentimentality in this love for birds, but a resolve, in the midst of the drabness of a materialistic age, to preserve what beauty remained to man. It was a most intense reaction against his own youthful callousness; but he did not attempt, as has been suggested, to conceal his early career as a collector. In one of his last books he still wrote quite openly of those days "when I was a sportsman and collector, always killing things". For it was true that, at this age, his natural compassion was in abeyance to ambition, and throughout the letters he cultivated the same careful professional sangfroid which in years to come drove him to fury when practised by others. It was only when he had gained confidence and wisdom that he allowed freedom to those sensitive feelings from which his greatness as a writer could grow. Like Grey Owl, the beaver trapper, he would turn then in horror from destruction to eloquent and passionate protectiveness.

A week later he wrote a second time to Dr. Sclater, giving a detailed account of twelve birds found in the river fringe; and this was followed on January 28th, 1870, by an astonishing letter consisting in the main of an attack on the godlike Darwin. To illustrate his theory that "natural selection" might allow a creature's structure to alter, so as to form a new species, the great naturalist had cited one of the South American woodpeckers, the Carpintero, as having become adapted to life on the pampas "where not a tree grows".

"However close an observer that naturalist may be," wrote Hudson (in that tone of grave emphasis, not devoid of glee, with which an undergraduate might bring a nodding tutor up to the mark), "it was not possible for him to know much of a species from seeing perhaps one or two individuals, in the course of a rapid ride across the pampas." He went on:

"The perusal of the passage I have quoted from, to one acquainted with the bird referred to, and its habitat, might induce him to believe that the author purposely wrested the truths of Nature to prove his theory; but as his 'Researches', written before the theory of Natural Selection was concieved—abounds in similar misstatements, when treating of this country, it should rather, I think, be attributed to carelessness"—to the same cause, in fact, as the frankly admitted errors of Hudson himself. The letter went on to describe the tree-shaded districts of the province, where the species might be seen "climbing the trees, resting on his stiff and frayed tail feathers, and boring the bark with his bill as other woodpeckers do." It continued:

"But his favourite resort is to the solitary Ombú, a tree found over a great extent of the plains of Buenos Ayres; this tree attains a considerable size"; and then, as though he had lifted his head from the page to gaze out at the hot midsummer plain: ". . . there is one within fifty paces of the room I am writing in. . . . This very tree was, for many years, a breeding place for several Carpinteros. . . . Twenty years ago, which is as far back as my recollection extends, it was rather a common bird, but has now become very rare."

It was a remarkable tribute to Hudson's growing prestige in the eyes of Dr. Sclater that this passage (although somewhat modified) was printed with the rest in the *Proceedings*. Darwin himself, in a subsequent issue, paid him the compliment of writing a long reply, which, with Olympian calm, admitted error. He mildly enquired, however, whether the woodpecker might not have different habits in different districts (an argument which Hudson himself was to use when challenged to defend an account of the American puma) and quoted the eighteenth-century ornithologist, Don Felix de Azara, in support of his own description.

Yet another writer—one who had lived in the country, and had not contented himself with "a rapid ride" across it—bears out Darwin's opinion of the pampas as comparatively treeless. Writing in 1868, Thomas J. Hutchinson, British Consul at Rosario, said: "I consider that it is a very criminal thing for any writer to represent a country as possessing elements (which) do not exist. Who can trust ancient authors about the River Plate territories, when a seeker for information reads (in 'Account of the Abipones', from the Latin of Martin Dobrizhoffer, 1822)—'The land round about the city of Buenos Ayres for near two hundred leagues is a *well-wooded* plain. . . .' For the prairie plains of Buenos Ayres camp, from its port to the other side of the continent, bear no more evidence of ever having been wooded, than you have in the present day of strawberry beds on the Goodwin Sands."

Clearly, to the two English writers, the scattered groves and plantations where Hudson found such variety of wild life simply did not appear as woods at all.

Again, writing to Dr. Sclater on May 19th, 1870, Hudson quoted a passage on the same controversy from *Habit and Intelligence*, by a writer named Murphy.

"Nor can any one doubt that our woodpeckers' feet are adapted to climb trees; yet there is a woodpecker

inhabiting the Pampas of South America where trees
are unknown. The inference is obvious, and I think
certain . . . that the woodpeckers of the Pampas are
a colony of woodpeckers which have strayed away from
their aboriginal forests. . . . In this case the species
has become modified by its new habitat."

Hudson's succinct comment ran: "It will but little
affect the theories of Messrs. Darwin and Murphy,
that one of their numerous statements should be dis-
proved; it is but a leaf plucked from the giant tree in
whose shadow they sit—into whose shadow, perhaps,
all men must come and sit with them forever—but
as to this great question, wether root and branch be
sound or rotten, I presume not now to hazard a con-
jecture. But why should so much stress be laid on
this fable of a scansorial bird living on the ground?
If it was true, and the bird, transported by some
accident to a country destitute of trees, was obliged
to feed, roost and breed on the ground, I do not see
that it would lend any great favor to the theories of
the above mentioned gentlemen, unless it was proved
that it *had become modified* in its structure by its new
habitat, an assertion for which Mr. Murphy has no
authority."

As his papers continued to be read to meetings of
the Society in London, and to appear in its chronicle,
Hudson probably took more pains to improve his
spelling and punctuation. His style certainly gained in
assurance, while its spirited tone and descriptive power
(as the last vivid quotation shows) bore already the
stamp of the future writer. Sometimes a passage would
be marred by awkwardness of syntax and punctuation,
as in an account of a swarm of spiders: ". . . so numerous were they, that they continually baulked each

other in their attempts to rise in the air, there being a breeze blowing, as soon as one threw out its web it would be entangled in that of another: both spider would immediately seem to know the cause of the trouble for they would run angrily together, each trying to drive the other off." Yet, in the twelve long letters making up this series (each carefully copied in ink on flimsy writing-paper, the capital letters ornamented with flourishes) the fluent grace of his mature essays showed itself more and more clearly. Characteristic is a description of the effect of cold weather on a bird of the province: "The Urraca is in Winter a miserable bird, and appears to suffer more than any other creature from cold. In the evening, the flock, usually composed of from ten to twenty individuals, gathers on a thick branch of a tree sheltered from the wind, the birds crowding close together for warmth, and some of them roosting perched on the backs of their fellows. I once saw six birds roosting in this manner, two of them resting on the tree perched on the branch, and one on their backs, so that they formed a perfect pyrimid. . . . In the morning if fair, the flock betakes itself to some large tree on which the sun shines, and settles on the outermost twigs on its Eastern side, each bird with its wings drooping and its back turned towards the sun. In this attitude so spiritless, but denoting great sagasity—they spend an hour or two, warming their blood, and drying the dew from their scanty dress. During the day they bask much in the sun, and towards night may be again seen on the sunny side of a hedge or tree warming their backs in the last rays."

Then, to contradict the mood of this affectionate description, one finds him writing: "I have just become acquainted with a bird never before, I think, obtained in this region—the *Upucerthia dumetoria*. A pair of these birds (male and female) appeared in a field near my house this winter; and a month after first seeing them I succeeded in shooting both."

When a great storm flooded his friend's house in Buenos Aires, Hudson suffered a great personal misfortune, in the loss of his whole collection of birdskins, "one hundred species of passerine birds collected in this State, some of them never before obtained here, and others probably unknown to naturalists", as he told Dr. Sclater. The reference, in writing to his correspondent, was brief, but he could hardly have seen such a loss without bitterness. Yet this, too, was characteristic of the way in which his life was changing: the ties of the past fading with the deaths of his parents, the dividing of his father's property, and this destruction of the results of nearly a decade of work: the future beckoning to him from other lands.

However, his work in South America was not yet done. In that year of 1870, as autumn gave place to the June winter of the region, the mystery of migration began to fascinate him. His thoughts turned to the journey he chiefly longed to make, to the mysterious wilderness of Patagonia. In September, when winter visitors were about to leave the district once more for their nesting grounds in Patagonia, he was writing: "Most anxiously do I wait an opportunity of learning something from observation of the ornithology of that country"; and going on to list and describe these Patagonian species visiting the province.

Already his intention had crystallized into plans for the journey. Now, in 1871, in fulfilment of the old childish wish to follow the migrants southward, he set out at last on what were to remain the most memorable of his travels. As an Englishman might go to Egypt or Africa, beguiled by the hope of hearing the cuckoo's note and watching the swallows in a setting so different from the English countryside, so he pictured himself again finding Magellanic geese, hawks, ibis and plover, in the fertile valley of the Rio Negro.

The plan to make a wide and detailed study of these migrants failed to some extent, at least in Hudson's ambitious estimation. Landing on a desolate shore after a narrow escape from shipwreck, he met within a few weeks with an accident to the knee which forced him to lie helpless for a time, and later restricted him to hobbling about with a stick, or to sitting gossiping with his new friends, unable to venture far into wild country. By the time the wound was healed he found that either the mild climate, or simply the pleasant habit of idleness, had blunted some of his first enthusiasm. Nevertheless, these "idle days in Patagonia" brought him a hundred varied adventures: while, as he later found, the thoughts and ideas bred from the desert solitude left a deep and enduring mark on his spirit.

Although the journey thus proved different to the one he had imagined, it was marked by collector's triumphs which would have been more than satisfying to one of lesser zeal and vitality. Chief among these was the discovery of the new species, that black tyrant-bird which was to bear his name. Describing another adventure, he wrote of his discovery of a flock of flamingos in a lagoon, and of how he crept up to the rushes bordering the water "in a fever of delighted excitement—not that flamingos are not common in that district, but because I had noticed that one of the birds before me was the largest and loveliest flamingo I had ever set eyes on, and I had long been anxious to secure one very perfect specimen". He fired, the bird was retrieved at length from the treacherous mud by a clever old sporting dog belonging to his host, and the rapturous account continued: "Never had I seen such a splendid specimen! It was an old cock bird, excessively fat, weighing sixteen pounds, yet Major had brought it out through this slough of despond without breaking its skin, or soiling its exquisitely beautiful, crimson, rose-coloured and faintly-blushing white plumage!"

Nor was Dr. Sclater to be disappointed of the promised report on the bird-life of this region. In March 1872 there arrived in London an essay "On the Birds of the Rio Negro of Patagonia", which was published the following month in the *Proceedings*. With a collection of birdskins sent to the Zoological Society there came also a letter from Hudson:

"I wrote a few days ago to inform Mr. Sclater that I had returned from Patagonia, and had determined to send him all the specimens, or at least duplicates of all the species collected, as well as notes on them. I now forward them; and as I cannot here learn the names of some of the species of which I am most anxious to speak, I have numbered these. . . . My observations have been confined to the valley of the Rio Negro. . . . I advanced altogether not much over a hundred miles from the sea. I met with 126 species altogether, but of these 93 are also found in the Buenos Ayrean pampas, 33 being confined to Patagonia.

"I engaged 10 or 12 Indians, by offering a liberal reward, to hunt for me; they went out several times, but failed to capture a single bird."

This essay is chiefly memorable for its happy descriptions of the songs and notes of the birds detailed.

One would like to know whether members of the scientific gatherings at which they were read enjoyed or deprecated such imaginative passages as—"When the profound stillness of midnight yet reigns and the thick darkness that precedes the dawn envelopes earth, suddenly the noise of this little bird is heard wonderfully sweet and clear" . . . "I have often observed that when a bird, while singing, emits a few of these *new* notes, he seems surprised and delighted with them; for after a slight pause he repeats them again and again a vast number of times, as if to impress them on his memory". . . . "When I discovered that all the strains I had heard had issued from a single throat, how much was my wonder and admiration for the delightful performer increased!"

To this essay Dr. Sclater's note recorded: "It would appear that one or other of his predecessors was fortunate enough to obtain specimens of nearly all the birds peculiar to this district, leaving to Mr. Hudson only the little *Cnipolegus.*" This species (of which Hudson had sent four male specimens) was accordingly named after "its energetic discoverer": who had already been honoured by being made a Corresponding Member of the Zoological Society, giving him the right to add the letters C.M.Z.S. to his name.

Hudson's next contribution to the *Proceedings* was a long essay on the swallows of Buenos Aires. He had begun to write on this subject in the twelfth letter to Dr. Sclater, before the Patagonian journey, and while in Patagonia he had paid special attention to the different song-notes heard from different species. This article contained a striking passage of observation, unsurpassed, perhaps, in any of his later writings—an account of marauding swallows taking over the

great oven-shaped nests of oven-birds while still
in use.

"After the swallows have taken up their station near
the oven," he wrote, "they occasionally fly towards
and hover about it . . . by and by they take to flying
at the mouth of the coveted home; this is a sort of
declaration of war, and marks the beginning of hos-
tilities. The oven-birds, full of alarm and anger, rush
upon and repel them as often as they approach; they
retire, but not discomfited, and warbling out their
gay notes in answer to the outrageous indignant
screams of the *Furnarii*. . . . At length the lawless
invaders, grown bolder, no longer fly from the master
of the house: desperate struggles now frequently take
place at the entrances. . . . Victory at last declares
itself for the aggressors, and they busy themselves
carrying in materials for the nest, screaming their
jubilant notes all the time, as though in token of
triumph. Thus are the brave and industrious oven-
birds often expelled from the house that cost them so
much labour to build. . . . When unable to drive the
oven-birds by force from their citadel, they fall back
on a dribbling system of warfare, and keep it up till
the young birds leave it, when they take possession
before the nest has grown cold."

In the next three years, several further papers were
to appear in the Society's journal, and it seemed now
to the naturalist that his footing in England was
secure and friendly, while his native land no longer
held him. He was thirty-three; he had little money—
not even, as yet, the sixth share in Daniel Hudson's
estate which would come to him after the younger
Daniel, as eldest son, should have been allotted his
portion; but this share, of which payment was delayed

until June 1874, he may have anticipated. And, even if he had little more than his fare to England, doubtless he felt that this need not worry him. He was Mr. William Henry Hudson, C.M.Z.S., an exile by two generations, and yet by no means unknown in the "land of his desire": an exile returning home.

So on April 1st, 1874, in Easter Week, he left the native land which he was never to see again; hearing, as the *Ebro* put to sea on her stormy voyage, the wistful note of his younger brother's parting words, that many were to echo in his later English years: "Of all the people I have ever known, you are the only one I don't know."

Chapter IV

The Stone Forest

THE LITTLE packet, under steam and sail, took more than a month to cross the Atlantic. As she drew nearer to England, Hudson's eagerness changed to impatience while he imagined the spring days passing, the time of bird-song and nesting reaching its peak, and himself still rolling at sea between the old life and the new. But his dream of taking up again the life of a naturalist, in all its freedom and simplicity, such as he had known on the pampas, began at once to meet with disillusionment and frustration that later made him smile wryly in recalling it.

He had made friends on board the *Ebro*, as he was always, wherever he went, to attract friends: one of these a student named Abel Pardo, and a future Senator of Buenos Aires, was in fact to prove a lifelong acquaintance, and to seek out Hudson whenever he returned to England in after years. These travelling companions expected Hudson to go on with them to London, and were surprised to find him ready to say goodbye at the dockside: for Hudson, in England at last and close to Gilbert White's countryside, wanted to be alone and to look for birds. The only companion he would have welcomed would have been one who could answer his questions. Instead, he found himself driving out into the country with a most persistant shipboard acquaintance who refused to be shaken off, declaring

72

himself interested in English farming methods. The stolid youth who drove them proved as ignorant as they. By Hudson's eager "What bird is that? What bird sang that note?" he was as bewildered as by the other's "I say, what crop is that?—Yes, but what sort of grass?"

He managed next day to give his exasperating friend the slip, and drove alone to Netley woods; but again he found himself at a loss without anyone to tell him anything of the birds he saw and heard. Wandering about Southampton and its surroundings, he tried now to plan his future. To reach England had been his aim, and this he had achieved. Nor was he disappointed. The green countryside, the bright soft light, seemed wonderful; even the smell of malt and hops in a Southampton street took on a magical tang, and seemed the essence of this "land of morning". But he must make a living, and clearly his best way to do so lay in contact with other "bird men", to whom he might be useful. In this spirit of naïve confidence he began to look for work, and, after staying for a time with the family of a South American friend at Malmesbury, he went to London.

Of his first day in the city he wrote a vivid description: "I put up at a City hotel, and on the following day went out to explore, and walked at random, never inquiring my way of any person, and not knowing whether I was going east or west. After rambling about for some three or four hours, I came to a vast wooded place where few persons were about. It was a cold wet morning in early May, after a night of incessant rain; but when I reached this unknown place the sun shone out and made the air warm and fragrant and the grass and trees sparkle with innumerable raindrops. Never grass and trees in their early spring foliage looked so vividly green, while above the sky was clear and blue

73

as if I had left London leagues behind. As I advanced farther into this wooded space the dull sounds of traffic became fainter, while ahead the continuous noise of many cawing rooks grew louder and louder. I was soon under the rookery listening to and watching the birds as they wrangled with one another, and passed in and out among the trees or soared above their tops. How intensely black they looked amidst the fresh brilliant green of the sunlit foliage! What wonderfully tall trees were these where the rookery was placed! It was like a wood where the trees were self-planted, and grew close together in charming disorder, reaching a height of about one hundred feet or more. Of the fine sights of London so far known to me, including the turbid, rushing Thames, spanned by its vast stone bridges, the cathedral with its sombre cloud-like dome, and the endless hurrying procession of Cheapside, this impressed me the most. The existence of so noble a transcript of wild nature as this tall wood with its noisy black people, so near the heart of the metropolis, surrounded on all sides by miles of brick and mortar and innumerable smoking chimneys, filled me with astonishment; and I may say that I have seldom looked on a scene that stamped itself on my memory in more vivid and lasting colours."

This was a happy introduction to the city where he was to live for fifty years; but his object in coming to London was probably to visit Dr. Sclater, who, when they lived thousands of miles apart, had given him so much encouragement. The acquaintance can hardly be said to have progressed on their meeting. He was later to collaborate with his learned friend in a book on Argentine birds; Sclater, also, was one of those who signed his naturalization papers when he took

British citizenship; yet in temperament they remained worlds apart.

The same proved true of his brief contact with John Gould, another ornithologist best known for a monograph on humming-birds, whom Hudson (perhaps at Dr. Sclater's suggestion) next went to see. Gould, a sick man, behaved badly at this meeting, mocking at the proud, shy young immigrant with his "pretensions" to some knowledge of birds, and his confessed ambition to write about them; and Hudson left with feelings of chagrin and contempt which he expressed in a satiric sketch so brutal that, having published it, he was afterward ashamed of its very truthfulness—a conflict between inbred courtesy and capacity for hatred which was characteristic.

Confidence was still further shaken by another encounter, this time with a bankrupt archaeologist, Chester Waters, who engaged him as a secretary: probably less for his secretarial aptitude than for his formidable looks. Waters was trying to live by the dubious means of tracing or inventing genealogies for Americans interested, like Hudson himself, in their family origins. However, as his house was in a constant state of siege from creditors and bailiffs, he could not leave it to carry on his affairs. Hudson therefore found himself involved in the drab makeshifts of Waters' existence, from which his wife and daughter had already fled: as, for instance, when food had to be tied to cords let down from upper windows, since he was unable to get back into the house without being followed. With his taste for odd situations, he might have found this amusing for a time; but he needed money, and Waters could not or would not pay his salary. The pair had fierce quarrels, Waters asserting with insolence, "It's no use asking me for money. I haven't any"—which was probably only too true. Finally, still unpaid, he threw a batch of papers in his employer's face and left, admitting defeat.

Eighteen years had passed since he first faced the problem of living. In those years he had travelled far, physically and mentally; his mind was stocked with ideas and experiences, and he had served his first apprenticeship both as naturalist and writer. But, as he was beginning to realise, his years of bird-collecting and even his Zoological Society papers had done little toward giving him any standing in England. Here he must start life over again: but he had not that practical streak which enabled Jefferies to become a competent newspaperman, nor, as yet, the academic patience and erudition which made it possible for Edward Thomas to earn a precarious living for his family from literary hackwork. Patience was a quality which ill became him. Yet now, in his own way, he tried to acquire it, and to discipline his talents into producing work which publishers and magazine editors would accept. In this he was sometimes untrue to himself, and his work uncharacteristic. From the outset, however, its merit was here and there recognized and rewarded—with publication, if not with anything more substantial. It is ironical that one of his admirers, praising him at the height of his success, was to declare, "Hudson writes as the grass grows." The grass in these years had already begun to grow, but the steed was brought near to starvation by this winter of hardship.

Looking back, he himself said once that his life ended when he left the pampas, and in one sense this was true: England was to change him, as time passed, from the vigorous and high-spirited young horseman of the plains to a gentle bearded giant in a Norfolk jacket, his field-glasses slung across his shoulders, cycling quietly along the dusty lanes of the home counties. It was a change which he resented with all his being. Yet in another sense he never left the pampas. Even when he wrote of England, his mind was constantly retracing those wide plains and sifting the richness of his youthful life; and the boy who had lingered about the streets of Buenos Aires, the youth who had listened to talk beside estancia fires or under shady ombu trees, became now the shabby keen-eyed onlooker, himself of striking appearance, who watched the men and women of the London streets as intently as the magpies in St. James's Park or the swans of Hackney marshes.

London, for him as for Jefferies, was not always the "unfriendly wilderness". Often it seemed to him as "a desert of tar and macadam", or a great stone forest teeming with life, and there was that in both desert and forest to match his moods. It was the London of which Professor Trevelyan has written: "To millions the divorce from nature was absolute, and so, too, was the divorce from all dignity and beauty and significance in the wilderness of mean streets in which they were bred, whether in the well-to-do suburb or the slum. The new education and the new journalism were both the outcome of these surroundings and partook of their nature. The race bred under such conditions might retain many sturdy qualities of character, might even with better food and clothing improve in physique, might develop sharp wits and a brave, cheery, humorous attitude to life, but its imaginative powers must necessarily decline, and the stage is set for the gradual standardization of human personality."

Hudson, often with pity and anger, was aware of this, and from such awareness sprang the two channels of his life's work—his writings and his efforts for the protection of wild life. *The sense of beauty,* he wrote, *is God's best gift to the human soul;* and this was the faith which ("religious atheist" as he now declared himself) he tried to express.

His first novel, *Ralph Herne,* was an attempt to describe the life of a doctor in Buenos Aires during the yellow fever epidemic of 1872. He himself had been in Patagonia at that time, and so could give only a secondhand account; and it was not until 1888 that the editor of a magazine called *Youth* accepted the story as a serial. His next attempt, a massive work which he entitled *The History of the House of Lamb,* was far more valuable, since he now tried to put down some of his actual experiences. It was written on the leaves of countless small pocket notebooks: appropriately so, since he had no home, and must have worked wherever he found himself—on park benches, in libraries, in London lodgings, or at the homes of friends whom he visited in Scotland and in Gloucestershire—and carried his manuscripts about with him. Even when pruned down to the fragment which became his first published book, *The Purple Land that England Lost,* this script stood two and a half feet high, while the spirit of the writer whirled through its pages like a pampas wind. Ten years were to pass, however, before the book appeared; and these were hard years of trial, exercise and experiment, with little to show at the end.

First of his experiments to be printed was a short essay "Wanted—A Lullaby", by "Maud Merryweather", which appeared in December 1874 in Cassell's *Family Magazine.* Here he condemns the frivolous mamma who, having quietened her infant with "narcotics", sails out to adorn the social scene, leaving the unfortunate baby alone in a drugged sleep. He regrets that there should be no national lullaby to compare with the Spanish mother's crooning, and speaks of other cradle songs heard in South America. The theme has momentary interest here: ". . . that of the Tehuelches, the wandering tribe of Southern Patagonia, pleased me most, and is a monotonous song, the words expressive of maternal fondness and delight in the beauty of the 'swart papoose' "—and he then demands, "Is it not that the artificial life of our times has the effect of weakening the genuine mother-nature?" However, it appears that even his own mother had failed to find the perfect lullaby: she would sing her children to sleep with the hymn, "There is a happy land", which was "not a restful tune". With the right air, he maintains, a child may be sung to sleep with any words, "even if profound and obscure as any Mr. Browning writes"; yet the right words would be an advantage, and he suggests that some English poet might perform this service for English children.

The essay includes a ballad, to be sung to a Spanish air; although he modestly explains that the words would be suitable only for the children of his own land. These verses, in their plaintive lilt, recall others which he used in *The Purple Land*.

> Once an Indian mother
> Left alone her child
> In the rushes lying
> Sleeping in the wild.
>
> When she came to seek him
> Loud and clear she sung
> As a bird comes flying
> Singing to her young.

Once an Indian warrior
In the desert found
All alone, a baby
Sleeping on the ground.

In his breast he hid it
And he fled away
Fled o'er hill and valley
Fled by night and day.

And the mother mourned it
As the ewe doth mourn
For the lamb the eagle
To the hill hath borne. . . .

In such tentative flights, the future writer of the
South American romances was trying his wings; as,
at the same time, the future author of *Nature in Downland* and *A Shepherd's Life* was shaping his course in
such work as a long, factual essay on the rails of the
Argentine, published two years later in the Zoological
Society's *Proceedings*.

It had been a fateful two years, hope alternating with
loneliness. He had begun to write in earnest and to
read widely. Entranced as he was by all music, he
went to the opera, and found the human voice almost
as moving as the songs of birds; and in this third year
of his English life he married a singer, Emily Wingrave, "because", he declared, "her voice moved
me as no voice had ever done before, though I had heard
all the great operative warblers of that time, Patti
included".

This was a cool and simple explanation for a marriage
that in later years seemed to many of his friends
lamentable. Slight, fragile, golden-haired Emily Wingrave was said to have enjoyed triumphs in concert
and opera in Paris, and to have appeared in London

at the Crystal Palace with Sims Reeves and other great singers of her day. But now she no longer sang, except among the guests at a boarding-house which she kept in Leinster Square, Bayswater, where Hudson had gone to stay. Fifteen or twenty years older than he, and with a background of life so different, it was scarcely surprising if she had little understanding of him or of his work; still less surprising if after enduring years of poverty and struggle, she came to resent a success which emphasised the incongruous element in their marriage.

Yet it would be hard, after all, to picture Hudson "suitably" married. Ford Madox Hueffer imagined that there was "no doubt and no reason for preserving secrecy as to the fact that Hudson had once, far away and long ago, nourished an intolerable passion for a being who had a beautiful voice and sang from the gleaming shadows of the green mansion of an ombú " : and, though he himself never spoke or wrote directly of this, it seems that with a beautiful, wild-hearted, elusive being such as Rima—if such a woman could exist—he might for a time have been happy. Yet now, though he might have returned to his native land, he chose to live in Bayswater; and experience proved that, while writing brought him little enough, he was not fitted for any other work. The bond between affections and economics—not least among the troubles of this proud and angry man—had defeated others before him; but with Emily Wingrave he found a home, sympathy in a lonely time, companionship which in those years was protective and unexacting, and a chance to devote himself to the slow unfolding of his gifts: something of the security of the mother-and-child relationship which, as appears from his writings, was so often in his mind. For all its pathos, it was a kind and timely marriage, and when it had lasted for forty-five years he wrote:

"It is kindness that counts in the end—the feeling for another that outlives short-lived passion. Now I was never in love with my wife, nor she with me. But we became friends. Once, reading a book of mine, *Afoot in England*, she asked me why I always spoke of her as my companion and not my wife. [His reply had been that a wife might not be a companion.] And after these eight years of her illness, and after we have been so much apart, I feel that the one being who knew me and whom I knew as I can know no other, has left me very much alone."

Spiritually alone, in this strange partnership, he must always have been; yet this solitude, like the desert of Patagonia, quickened his thoughts, and gave life to the people crowding his imagination and to the spirited debates of his mind. Now, too, he was fortunate in finding a congenial and nimble-minded friend to become his confidant.

It was on an evening of late summer in 1880 that Morley Roberts rang the bell of No. 11 Leinster Square and gazed with interest at the stranger who answered his enquiry. Unconscious power seemed the keynote of this man's personality, together with an impressive and warming friendliness.

"His height was about six feet three inches when he stood upright, which he rarely did," Roberts recalled. "He wore a short cropped beard and an untrimmed moustache: his hair in his youth was dark brown. . . . His eyes were more or less hazel and deeply set, with heavy brow ridges and well-marked eyebrows: his nose, large and prominent and by no means symmetrical.

His complexion was sallow, and his ears, though well-formed, as large in proportion as his hands and feet. . . .
But it was Hudson's whole aspect that showed the man.
It marked him with a rare stamp. It was at once kindly and formidable. He looked like a half-tamed hawk which at any moment might take to the skies and return no more to those earth-bound creatures with whom he had made his temporary home. His sight was keen: his curiosity insatiable. He was as much the field-naturalist in London as in the country. In town, for beasts and birds he substituted the whole race of man. This gave him his air of interested armed detachment. . . .

"Though many photographs of him are good and often better than good, none will ever see again Hudson's brooding smile, suffused with humour, nor catch the light in him which warmed and illuminated his talk. His power and size, the roundness of his skull, its shape and index, showed there was much in him of Beaker ancestry, those powerful men with round skulls and big noses, whose round (or long) barrows with drinking beakers in them are found from Torquay to Caithness, men whose descendants are still strong, men who 'get there', who do things and are not born to be hewers of wood and drawers of water. . . .
With good health he would have been a marvel of strength."

Himself a traveller and a future writer, Roberts had come across impressive and ambitious men before, and found them in the end too often "nothing but squeezed lemons with the juice gone". But no such disillusionment followed his first meeting with Hudson. Though many years younger, Roberts so won his confidence that in time he would talk to him of his work and his hopes, of *The Purple Land* (some of which he altered at Roberts' suggestion) and of his essays and verse. It was when he read an essay called "The Settler's Recompense", published in 1883 in a little literary journal, *Merry England*, that he realised Hudson's latent greatness. Later rewritten as a chapter for *Idle Days in Patagonia*, the essay described the war with nature awaiting the hopeful immigrant, and ended in the true Hudson vein of proud philosophy, if not of perfect syntax:

"The man who finishes his course by a fall from his horse, or is swept away while fording a swollen stream, has spent as bright, useful and happy, if not happier, life than he who dies of apoplexy in his counting-house or dining-room. . . . Certainly, the dreary refrain concerning the vanity of all earthly things has been less frequent on his lips."

This noble plainsman in him, this sweeping contempt for all that was petty in civilization, captivated Morley Roberts, as later it was to captivate the high-spirited Cunninghame Graham. He had become an eager caller at the Leinster Square house: though always it seemed to him dreadful to find Hudson dining at that table, opposite the faded Emily and among typical boarding-house dwellers who could neither understand nor interest him. There he would sit, a dragon in shallow waters, brooding and silent, or suddenly flashing into talkative and sardonic humour in response to his friend. Then he would get up to squeeze and drink fresh lemon-juice at the sideboard, thinking this brought some relief to the rheumatic pains which always tormented him; and he and Roberts would go out to sit for hours under the plane-trees in the city dusk.

It was perhaps at night that the longing for the pampa sometimes overcame him; when, thinking of the wide windy plains, until he fancied that he heard again the lowing of cattle and the plaintive note of the partridge, tears would come to his eyes. Confined in the airless city, he suffered then the anguish of the caged eagle, of the shabby crested screamer in Regent's Park, and all creatures accustomed to wide horizons. But with Roberts, who had travelled widely, he could share memories of deserts and plains; and his friend would listen with sympathy as he described the gaucho's skill as horseman, with the lasso and in the game of El Pato; or his own sensations when, on those far-off evenings under the southern stars, he loved to lie prone on his horse's back as it galloped, feeling himself translated by the swift movement into a strange new element between earth and sky. Roberts in turn could kindle his interest with tales of the Australian plains. Hudson as yet had seen little of England, and Roberts, who had lived as a child in several counties, would tell him too of the Sussex downs, of Wiltshire and Salisbury plain (remembered from his boyhood reading) and the wild coast of Cornwall: finding him ready to love all parts of the country where there were cottages, woodlands and birds.

At this time he was writing a long poem, "The London Sparrow", to be printed in 1883 in *Merry England*: the same paper which, with its perceptive Editor Wilfred Meyrell, only four years after, made literary history in receiving the desperate last plea of another London wanderer, Francis Thompson. This poem, which he read aloud to Roberts page by page, was written in blank verse like his early loves, the *Seasons* and *The Farmer's Boy*. It followed a theme beloved by exiles to the city—the revengeful idea, part fantasy, part prophecy, which Richard Jefferies was then exploring in his story *After London*. Hudson began by expressing his longing for the wild, as he spoke to the intrepid sparrow:

> A hundred years it seemeth since I lost thee
> O beautiful world of birds, O blessed birds.
> I from such worlds removed to this sad world
> Of London we inhabit now together. . . .
>   a desert desolate
> Of fabrics gaunt and grim and smoke-begrimed
> By goblin misery haunted; scowling towers
> Of cloud and stone, gigantic tenements
> And castles of despair . . .

Comparing this world with the country he had known, where

>   reedy and vast
> Stretch ibis—and flamingo-haunted marshes,

he goes on to praise the sparrow:

>   Never yet
> In thy companionship of centuries
> With man in lurid London didst regret
> Thy valiant choice—yea, even from the time
> When all its low-roofed rooms were sweet with scents
> From summer fields, where shouting children plucked
> The floating lily from the reedy Fleet,
> Scaring away the timid water-hen . . .

and sees it at last remaining as "Nature's one witness" in the city, when

>   the murmuring sound
> Of human feet unnumbered, like the rain
> Of summer pattering on the forest leaves
> In everlasting silence dies away.

In the same nostalgic mood he described his longing for the wings of a seagull to fly away:

> Many a heron-haunted stream
> And many a plain I'd pass,
> A thousand, thousand flowers behold
> Strew all the wayside grass.

These verses, entitled "In the Wilderness", were also printed in *Merry England*. The same editor took a third poem, "Gwendoline", which shows even more clearly how little his gifts were suited to the form of verse:

> Like a streamlet dark and cold
> Kindled into fiery gold
> By a sunbeam swift that cleaves
> Downward through the curtained leaves—
>
> So this darkened life of mine
> Lit with sudden joy would shine;
> And to greet thee I would start
> With a great cry in my heart.

The Purple Land that England Lost, published in the same year as "Gwendoline", reaches a standard incomparably higher in thought, feeling and technical skill. But, although in 1885 he was forty-four years old, he had not yet found his bearings as a writer, nor made up his mind how best to use his knowledge and talents. It was for this reason that he delighted in the company of Morley Roberts. Intensely ambitious, with his mind full of plans for the books he wanted to write, Hudson needed the practice and stimulus of debate to give form to his ideas. His processes of mind, Roberts declared, had a "certain stateliness of motion" in talk, and to this the youthful confidence and

eloquence of his friend made a happy foil. Their long
debates on the instincts of wild cattle and horses, on
red rags and bulls, on birds' displays of singing and
dancing, on hereditary fear in birds, on how mosquitoes
fed when they could not suck human blood—these,
and many other topics, bore fruit; first in essays which
were accepted by the *Field* and other papers, and later
in *The Naturalist in La Plata*, whose chapters carried
question and answer further. Many of these theories,
such as the idea of animism and the instinct of bird
migration, had been since childhood a source of ardent
interest to Hudson, and in his last books and letters
he would still pursue them with increasing fervour
and insight.

All his life he was haunted by the idea of a mysterious
bird-woman: a kind of private fantasy springing from
a primitive legend or superstition heard in his early
years. A trace of it appears in the reason he gave
for his marriage—the charm of Emily Hudson's singing.
There is even an echo in his denunciations of "feathered
women"—those who followed the fashion of wearing
wings or plumes in their hats. The fancy was to touch
heights of beauty in the pitiful story of Rima, and of
horror in *Marta Riquelme*. In a tale written at this
time, "Pelino Viera's Confessions", the bird-woman
appears in demoniacal form, and is killed by her husband,
who tells the story while awaiting execution for her
murder: since, needless to say, he does not expect his
fantastic "confession" to be believed. This story—of
which one critic remarked that only a madman could
have written it—is told in a strain at once lurid and
cold-blooded; qualities which were retained, though
more subtly presented, in his later fiction. It was his
first story to be printed, appearing in 1883 in the

Cornhill Magazine and in the following year in the *Nación* of Buenos Aires. He also found a market in *Home Chimes*, described by the *Athenaeum* as being the ablest and best-written of the weekly penny miscellanies. The first volume, published in 1884, contained his second printed story, "Tom Rainger". This was set in Trinidad and was at least of sufficient merit to attract the notice of a fellow-writer, Coulson Kernahan, who recalled it after meeting Hudson at some literary gathering several years later.

Before leaving for America in the same year, Morley Roberts introduced Hudson to George Gissing. The pair had in common their love of books and of their profession as writers, but for Hudson it was not entirely a happy association. The grey realism and half-flippant bitterness of Gissing's outlook was intolerable to him. Gissing pretended to accept poverty and failure as inevitable, even amusing, and to look forward complaisantly to a future in Marylebone workhouse; a joke which Hudson failed to appreciate, since at times it seemed only too likely to become his own fate. It was not that Hudson lacked humour, but that his humour and his sense of values differed from those of Gissing, whose cockney facetiousness depressed him. His natural pride and integrity owed something both to his Celtic blood and to the Spanish influence of his early days. It was not for nothing that the phrase "Grand Seigneur" should have occurred to Coulson Kernahan on their first meeting; in outlook he was always an aristocrat, and, conscious of his own powers, he could not resign himself to the poverty and ob-scurity of this drab phrase of life. He and Gissing continued to meet, however, and to exchange letters. To Gissing, as to Kernahan, Hudson showed himself as an inspired interpreter of the Spanish literature he knew so well, encouraging Gissing to learn the language so that he might read *Don Quixote* in the original. The two also exchanged their own books as these appeared. Hudson's work, so different to his own, Gissing found pleasing; but, to Hudson, Gissing's books were always painful, since they too stressed poverty and reminded him of this second dark time in his life—the middle years of the 'eighties.

It was a time of such hardship and wretchedness that, as with the shadowed years of his youth, he could afterwards hardly bear to speak of it. The Leinster Square boarding-house failed, perhaps through Emily Hudson's mildness with defaulting guests. They opened another in Southwick Crescent, and here he went on writing while she struggled to keep a roof over their heads; but this too was a failure, and the pair found themselves in a single room in the suburb of Ravenscourt Park, trying to exist on the proceeds of his articles and of Emily's music-lessons. So desperately poor were they that, as he later grimly admitted, they lived for one week on a tin of cocoa and milk; an extremity which Galsworthy seems to have recalled, perhaps unconsciously, when he came to record the youthful hardships of Philip Bosinney, in his *Man of Property*. Cut off from the countryside, Hudson felt that he was not properly alive. His one source of happiness was in looking from their window at the green and shady wilderness of Ravenscourt Park, which he was to describe so gratefully in *Birds in London*. Here in spring he could see celandines and bluebells in the long grass, and hear the song of the willow-wren; while in winter the missel-thrush sang from the green cedars and leafless elms. The park was then part of a private home, so that he could not even walk there; but he remembered it with gratitude as the only beautiful thing in his life at that period.

To Morley Roberts he spoke long afterwards of his heart-breaking attempts to make a living: "When I had not a penny, and almost went down on my knees to editors, publishers and literary agents, I couldn't even get a civil word, and of ten—or perhaps twenty— MSS. sent nine or nineteen would be sent back. And now that I don't want the beastly money and care nothing for fame and am sick and tired of the whole thing they actually come to beg a book or article from me!"

The fate of *The Purple Land* (later to become one of his best-known books) was another hard blow; the more so as, in an era that showed such enthusiasm for the romances of Stevenson and Rider Haggard, it might well have been a success. The publishers, Sampson Low and Marston, had produced it in two handsome volumes, bound in light blue, with elegant decorations and pale green flowered end-papers; and, although he declared that no book had ever proved to be "the book he wanted to write", Hudson can scarcely have seen this long-awaited day of publication without some sense of achievement and high hopes for the future.

The full title was *"The Purple Land that England Lost:* Being the narrative of one Richard Lamb's adventure in the Banda Oriental in South America, as told by himself". It was characteristic of Hudson, with his deep reticence about personal affairs, that the "I" of his tales was never the "I" of his factual essays. Whenever he left the green plain of the naturalist, reporter or philosopher for the tropical forest of fiction, and began to examine emotions and experiences which the curious might interpret as his own, he had first to disguise himself by elaborately assuming another personality. The blue-eyed Richard Lamb, however, is never more than a lay figure, and his journey through the Purple Land is a mere pretext for stringing together a sequence of bizarre and spirited tales. The book is packed with material enough for half a dozen novels, and is peopled with crafty old plainsmen, bloodthirsty ruffians and beautiful women, usually in some measure of distress. The chapter headings—"Manuel, Also Called The Fox"—"A Ghastly Gift"—"Mystery of the Green Butterfly"—"Lock and Key and Sinners Three"—parody the swaggering gaiety, the grimness or light-hearted fancy of each anecdote. The book has been called passionate, but the dalliance of Richard Lamb seems hardly to justify this. Sentimentality redeemed by irony is rather the keynote of his adventures, and their idiom, "Tell me, dearest Dolores, can you forgive me?—How cruel destiny is to us!" But over and over again the tale shows his lively humour, his satiric gift and new felicity of language; as when he mockingly describes an opportunity missed:

"Love cometh up as a flower, and men and charming women naturally flirt when brought together. Yet it was hard to imagine how I could have started a flirtation and carried it on to its culminatory point in that great public room, with all those eyes on me: dogs, babes, and cats tumbling about my feet; ostriches staring covetously at my buttons with great vacant eyes; and that intolerable paroquet perpetually reciting, 'How the waters came down at Lodore' in its own shrieky, beaky, birdy, hurdy-gurdy, parrot language"; or in the chapter called "Tales of the Purple Land", when, after some tall fairy-stories had been told around a gaucho fireside, and received by the company without a shadow of disbelief, Lamb begins to speak of London: only to be snubbed with, "Remember that we were speaking of actual experiences, not inventing tales of black fogs and glass palaces."

The Purple Land is a young man's book. The thread by which it is put together is slight and careless, the love scenes artificial; yet many of its men, women and children, dogs, birds and snakes, wasps and fireflies, flowers and willows, are observed and drawn with the beautiful directness which Hudson had already mastered. There are passages which foreshadow the confidence and ease of his mature style. "We are all vainly seeking after happiness in the wrong way," he writes, in idealising the pastoral bliss, the "Liberty and Dirt", of a Scots exile and his family: "It was with us once and ours, but we despised it, for it was only the old common happiness which Nature gives to all her children, and we went away from it in search of another grander kind of happiness which some dreamer —Bacon or another—assured us we should find. We had only to conquer Nature, find out her secrets, make her our obedient slave, then the earth would be Eden, and every man Adam and every woman Eve. We are still marching bravely on, conquering Nature, but how weary and sad we are getting! The old joy in life and gaiety of heart have vanished, though we do sometimes pause for a few moments in our long forced march to watch the labours of some pale mechanician seeking after perpetual motion and indulge in a little dry, cackling laugh at his expense."

But, despite such vitality and promise, the book was little noticed, and the first edition soon found its way to the remainder shelves: although fifty years later, when he had long been dead, a new edition of seventy-five thousand copies was sold out within two years. Most critics ignored it, perhaps discouraged by the title, which, as one complained, they found obscure and unmeaning. Also, it was not an easy book to classify at a glance; to be reviewed under "Travels and Geography" would scarcely recommend it to novel-readers. The only note of praise was sounded by Professor Keane, who wrote an enthusiastic review in the *Academy*. It appeared, however, that his favour had a personal bias: he himself, as he told Hudson, had travelled in his youth and had met with many adventures which, as it seemed to him, would make a wonderful romantic tale, if only he could weave them together. This he had tried and failed to do: but on reading *The Purple Land* he exclaimed to himself, "That's the book I have been trying so long to write and can't do it!" So he invited Hudson to dinner and make the ingenuous suggestion that the young author should take his notes and journals and write his book for him. Here, however, the incident ended: Hudson declining this task and pointing out that, if he were to attempt it, "it would read to him much as *The Purple Land* would to me if he had written that book after getting his facts from me". Nevertheless, heartened by the review and by this flattering proposal, he was able to accept more philosophically the disfavour of the *Saturday Review*. Another critic in the *Athenaeum* wrote tolerantly enough: "His various adventures are described with great spirit and gusto, giving what we can well believe to be a faithful, as it certainly is a vivid, portrayal of the spirit and character of the society into which he was thrown. The reader who has followed the author's fortunes so far will heartily wish him a prosperous ending to his troubles."

CHAPTER V

A Garret in Westbourne Park

HUDSON had not yet found any prosperous ending to his own troubles; but the worst years of his life were over when Morley Roberts returned from America at the end of 1886, to find the couple established in a house left to Mrs. Hudson on the death of a sister. After existing as they had done, under the shadow of starvation and pauperism, this legacy must have seemed like a sudden relenting of Providence. Tower House stands on the corner of St. Luke's Road in Westbourne Park: they found it a tall shabby mansion, melancholy in its disrepair, while the neighbourhood had seen better days. To visit the house now, to see the sombre trees at the door, to climb the flights of steep stairs and look out at the house-tops of Westbourne Park—to remember that from his garret window Hudson once fed his tame pigeons and sparrows, and in this room endured for years the "ever-lasting brain-worrying noises" of the traffic below—cannot fail to make one regret that, whatever his reason, he should have resigned himself for the rest of his life to this home.

The paradox of his marriage is matched by the strangeness of that resignation. Morley Roberts suggested that Emily Hudson clung to her property and would not part with it or live elsewhere so long as her health lasted; and, for all her devotion to her husband, she was probably capable of such obstinacy,

95

and little influenced by aesthetic notions which had no place in her world. But, as success came at last, his friends deplored the "cracked belfry" where they found their eagle imprisoned. They deplored too the boarding-house relics that furnished the rooms, where the only gleam of colour was a glass case holding his books: the ugly horse-hair circular settee, the commonplace pictures and china, "lace" curtains and ugly anti-macassars, and sofas "with the leather peeling off, hanging in flaps like the wattles round the neck of a vulture", as Violet Hunt wrote in exasperation. Why, he was asked, could he not move to the country, or even to a more congenial district of London? In 1889, indeed, one of his elder brothers begged him to return to the Argentine. Hudson had sent one of the three brothers, living in Buenos Aires, a copy of *The Purple Land*; it was passed on to another, in the city of Cordova, in the western province. This was almost certainly Edwin, who in boyhood had given Hudson such shrewd and affectionate advice, and who now wrote: "Why are you staying on in England, and what can you do there? I have looked at your romance, and find it not unreadable, but this you must know is not your line—the one thing you are best fitted to do. Come back to your own country and come to me here in Cordova. The woods and sierras and rivers have a more plentiful and interesting bird life than that of the pampas and Patagonia. Here I could help you and make it possible for you to dedicate your whole time to observation of the native birds and fauna generally." Hudson commented: "I read the letter with a pang, feeling that his judgement was right: but the message came too late; I had already made my choice, which was to remain for the rest of my life in this country of my ancestors, which had become mine." So England held him: despite his sufferings, the part where he had first touched English soil remained to him "my beloved Southampton". And, though the slow change in his fortunes made it possible at length to escape for long periods from London, he would not make his home elsewhere; partly because he liked to feel himself within reach of editors and publishers, with whom he insisted on dealing personally, refusing the help of literary agents. As for Tower House and its trappings, they were Emily's affair, and he did not see them; work, books and friends absorbed his thoughts while he was in town, and in his heart he thought of such a village as Martin, in Wiltshire— "the lovely, remote and peaceful place"—as his true home. It may be also that (even if Mrs. Hudson had agreed to leave) such a decision would have cost him more time and effort than, at any point in his career, he cared to spend. There was in him, too, a deep-rooted independence which perhaps helped to keep him in Westbourne Park when he might, for instance, have become Roberts' neighbour in Chelsea. In his un-fashionable district he was safe from casual callers, and in later years this was no small consideration.

But the books were not yet written which would bring indignant admirers to criticise Tower House; now it was a refuge to which he went thankfully. Asking little, he had been given the little he asked: bread to eat, a roof over his head, time to watch the seasons and to do his work.

They took for themselves the garret floor (although the long climb can hardly have been helpful to the spells of "palpitation, dizziness, nervelessness and general imbecility" from which Hudson suffered) not, as he grimly declared, for the sake of the purer air at that level, but because the lower floors brought more substantial rents. Here he corrected the proofs of his new book, *A Crystal Age*, while Emily Hudson, free now from active boarding-house management and the heavier anxieties of poverty, arranged her house-keeping and her music-lessons; and, when her own voice failed, taught Morley Roberts to sing for Hudson the simple airs and ballads he loved to hear. The hardest struggle was past, but still prosperity was delayed. Their one means of escape was in occasional country rambles, when Emily trudged with him through Sussex, Surrey, Hampshire and Berkshire, or sat in village lodgings while he searched for the Dartford warbler, picked up adders to measure their length, watched nesting birds, and mixed himself up, as he put it, in the affairs of weasels, voles, squirrels, stag-beetles, snipe and peewits. This was the period of which he wrote:

"The walks, at a time when life had little or no other pleasure for us on account of poverty and ill-health, were taken at pretty regular intervals two or three times a year. It all depended on our means; in very lean years there was but one outing. It was impossible to escape altogether from the immense unfriendly wilderness of London simply because, albeit 'unfriendly', it yet appeared to be the only place in the wide world where our poor little talents could earn us a few shillings a week to live on. Music and literature! but I fancy the nearest crossing-sweeper did better, and could afford to give himself a more generous dinner every day. It occasionally happened that an article sent to some magazine was not returned, and always after so many rejections to have one accepted and paid for with a cheque worth several pounds was a cause of astonishment, and was as truly a miracle as if the angel of the sun had compassionately thrown us down a handful of gold. And out of these little handfuls enough was sometimes saved for the country rambles at Easter and Whitsuntide and in the autumn."

The slenderness of their means may be measured from the fact that, writing to Emily from the country when she had stayed at home, he once described lodging in a cottage where the woman gave him "big fires, three or four meals a day and every luxury she could get"—for a pound a week: yet even this he could rarely afford.

Morley Roberts would sometimes accompany him, and the two went together to Cookham Dean, the Thames-side village where Hudson was making notes for *Birds in a Village*, and where Roberts had the happiness of pointing out the long-sought grasshopper-warbler to him. At Shoreham in Sussex, then a cheerful little sea-port town beloved of painters, they had a memorable adventure, saving three young women from drowning. Here, too, Roberts observed in him a characteristic gesture—his greeting the sea by walking into the surf and scooping up a handful of water to drink, as though in tribute to Poseidon or whatever god he had first learned to pledge beside the Silver Sea.

Meanwhile, *A Crystal Age* had appeared. It was published anonymously, but the name of its author—as soon as he might be said to have a "name" as a writer—later became known. Like *The Purple Land*, it slowly acquired its admirers—among them Hilaire Belloc, who many years later declared that it was "the book he had read most often and liked best". *A Crystal Age* was a document from Hudson's personal "unknown country"—that country of the mind which most writers at times inhabit, and which now and again has been set down as a Utopia, an Erewhon, a Nowhere. This was no optimistic design for a future state, however, but simply a strange and beautiful fairy tale. The hero, Smith, finds himself suddenly in a new country where life has been shattered and remoulded nearer to Hudson's dream of pastoral felicity. The people of the dream live in fine houses, wear a loose and graceful kind of dress (the word "aesthetic", then at the height of its vogue, must have been in his mind as he wrote), eat fruit and herbs and honey, and spend their working hours in the fields or the "work-house" and their leisure in riding spirited horses about the countryside to enjoy the beauties of nature. Illness is looked on as a misdemeanour, and they survive far beyond the span of three score and ten years. Writing before the grisly reign of totalitarianism, Hudson could innocently model his state in part on the pattern of the beehive; each community having one Mother, a revered and highly privileged queen who alone has the power of bearing children. The community is headed, however, by the Father, whose status is that of a king: to compare his role to that of the drone in a hive would clearly be *lèse-majesté*.

The theme underlying this fantasy of a crystal age was that (as Hudson explained to Edward Garnett) "the sexual fury had burnt itself out". Until this end had been achieved, he suggested, "there could be no millennium, no rest, no perpetual peace"; but he allowed the human race unlimited time to reach that goal. This condition is implicit in the girl Yoletta's attitude to Smith, whose declarations of love she cannot understand; it is further explored in veiled terms in his conversations with the Mother; but the interest of *A Crystal Age* lies outside these somewhat sentimental and tedious exchanges. It is rather in such forthright Stevensonian passages as that listing his antipathies, "politics, religions, systems of philosophy, isms and ologies of all descriptions; schools, churches, prisons, poor houses; stimulants and tobacco"—and so on. These, he blithely hopes, will be consumed to ashes: thus the tale is a prose exercise developing the mood of his "London Sparrow".

The despised isms and ologies were at present personified in Dr. Sclater, his old friend of the Zoological Society, with whom he now collaborated in compiling a standard *Argentine Ornithology*. Having little of the tact which such a partnership demanded, he found the work from the first a source of exasperation and bitterness. All the antagonism of poet to pedant, and of outdoor to indoor naturalist, was aroused in their encounters. He could not fail to believe (as others were later to confirm) that his vivid descriptions of the birds which as a child he had worshipped, and as a young collector closely observed, gave life to a book which would otherwise have seemed to all but the strict scientist "a dusty heap of bones". Dr. Sclater, not unnaturally, failed to see anything of the kind, and took his own contribution far more seriously. Also, despite the obvious need of the younger man, he was less than magnanimous in the division of royalties.

Argentine Ornithology appeared in 1888, being styled "A Descriptive Catalogue by P. L. Sclater, M.A., Ph.D., F.R.S. With Notes On Their Habits by W. H. Hudson, C.M.Z.S., Late of Buenos Ayres". The first book on the subject since that of Don Felix de Azara a century before, its publication was obviously important in the world of ornithology. This was probably the work which first brought him the friendship of Sir Edward Grey (later Lord Grey of Fallodon) and Lady Grey; for the writer of the *Charm of Birds* would delight in the delicate and ardent feeling prompting his account of Glittering Humming-birds on the wing, of the Scarlet Tyrant with crest glowing like a live coal among green leaves, of the grinding sound and zig-zag swoop of a flock of Scissor-tails in their sunset flight, the cheerful ringing note of the Cardinal, and the Southern Crested Screamer rising in its immense spiral to "sublime aerial exercises", with cries "of a jubilant martial character that strongly affects the mind in that silent melancholy wilderness".

These descriptions were taken from notes made long ago on the pampas, and there appears sometimes an image of his cruder youthful style, as in the graphic comment on the Guira Cuckoo: "There is something ludicrous in the notes of these young birds, resembling as they do the shrill half-hysterical laughter of a female exhausted by over-indulgence in mirth." Yet he was never vague nor inexact: he had the scientist's honesty and respect for accuracy. Thus in his note on the Spur-winged Lapwing he wrote: "Marking the spot she rises from, it is easy to find the nest on the open level pampas. In the course of a morning's ride I have picked up as many as sixty-four eggs." Thirty years after, in writing his boyhood autobiography, he remembered that same spring day of 1854: "The nests I found that morning contained one or two and sometimes three eggs—very rarely the full clutch of four. Before midday I had got back with a bag of sixty-four eggs; and that was the largest number I ever gathered at one time."

The boy of thirteen whom he remembered riding in triumph across the plain with his booty would have taken the eggs home for the family breakfast table; but, in this later book, he qualifies the description by explaining that lapwings were to be found in great flocks in that part of the pampas, which had not then been overrun by bird-destroying immigrants. This whole question of protecting birds and their eggs, already of heartfelt interest to him, was to become more and more his chief concern. He was one of the pioneers of a movement just beginning in England, to secure more humane treatment both for wild and domestic creatures. From this time onwards there appeared in his books informative passages aimed deliberately at stirring the reader's conscience in this direction. Within a decade or so, such bodies as the Societies for the Protection of Birds and the Prevention of Cruelty to Animals, together with the Humane League, were to gain a strong following; then the Cruel Sports Bill found many supporters; and to Hudson's writings were added, in other spheres of animal protection, the eloquent plea of crusading books such as Anna Sewell's *Black Beauty*, an earlier tract which became a classic.

At this point, in the late 'eighties, the callous fashion which caused many of the world's most beautiful birds to be slaughtered, so that their wings and plumes might be worn on women's hats and gowns, was arousing thoughtful and sensitive men and women to opposition. They began to look about for allies, and meetings were held in London and suburban drawing-rooms. From these first protests were to come the Wild Bird Protection Acts and other protective legislative measures; followed later by educative schemes, in which Hudson took a close personal interest, and which included essay competitions held in elementary schools. One of the campaigners was a Mrs. Edward Phillips, at whose meetings in her Croydon house he became an honoured guest and sympathiser. In 1889 the Society for the Protection of Birds was formed, then consisting of women pledged to wear no feathers of any bird not killed for food, the ostrich excepted. In 1891 there appeared the first of a dozen pamphlets which Hudson wrote for the Society—*The Osprey or Egrets and Aigrettes*, and *Save the Herons*.

These could not have been published at a more fortunate moment. He was already known to many bird-lovers as co-author of *Argentine Ornithology*; now, in February 1892, came *A Naturalist in La Plata*, bringing his first taste of success. A second edition was printed in June, followed by a third, and within three years one thousand seven hundred and fifty copies had been sold. This success meant that his career was headed at last towards a brighter future, and incidentally it added greatly to the prestige of the new Society.

Stephen Spender writes in his autobiography: "There is something about the literary life which, although it offers the writer freedom and honour enjoyed by very few, at the same time brings him a cup of bitterness with every meal. There is too much betrayal, there is a general atmosphere of intellectual disgrace, writers have to make too many concessions in order to support themselves and their families, the successful acquire an air of being elevated into public figures and therefore having lost their own personalities, the unsuccessful are too spiteful and vindictive and cliquey, and even the greatest, when they are attacked, reveal themselves often as touchy and vain. I think that almost every writer secretly feels that the literary career is not worthy of the writer's vocation. For this vocation resembles that of the religious. . . . If success is corrupting, failure is narrowing. What a writer really needs is a success of which he then purges himself. The writer's life should, in fact, be one of entering into external things and then withdrawing himself from them."

This sensitive analysis might have been written with Hudson's career in mind; for it was the measure of his strength and sanity, as well as of his powerful egotism, that he allowed no breath of that corruption to touch his success when at last it came to him. Nor had his years of "concessions" narrowed him. Seven years were still to pass before, at the turn of the century, he found himself among the leaders of "the literary life"; but he was too wise, too keen-eyed, too simple, too great to be deflected by this any more than by hardship and failure. At sixty, as at fifteen, his cry was still *What do I want? What do I ask to have?* and his answer had not changed. To the end of his life he would continue to delight in action, in nature, in the lives, the minds, the beauty, the speech or singing voices of human beings and wild creatures, and then to withdraw into silence and solitude at intervals.

During those seven years he laid aside his stories to produce one volume after another of essays and records as a field naturalist—"bread and cheese books", as he termed them. A novel, *Fan, The Story of a Young Girl's Life*, had appeared in 1893 under the pseudonym "Henry Harford"; but this, though its early pictures of London poverty ring true, was otherwise a sterile production, far removed from the sparkle and impudence of *The Purple Land* or the imaginative waywardness of *A Crystal Age*. A hack text-book, *British Birds*, was published in 1895, and *Birds in London*— a much better book—in 1898: the latter, for all its detailed competence, a somewhat pathetic document in contrast with the grand scope of his South American work. He wrote several more pamphlets for the Bird Society—*Feathered Women*, *Letter to Clergymen*, *The Trade in Birds' Feathers*; and *Lost British Birds*, which led him into conflict with Alfred Newton, "old conservative academic Newton, Professor of Zoology for half a century at Cambridge, the doyen of the Ornithological world, who glared at me, an Argentine, who dared to come to England and write about birds!" (After his death this pamphlet was expanded from his notes into the little book *Rare, Vanishing and Lost British Birds*; the editor being Linda Gardiner, a Secretary of the Society, who had been his friend, and whose advice he had valued, for twenty years.)

Always diffident about his work while it was in progress, he might have been discouraged from ever finishing another story had he not at this time come under a new and refreshing influence. The South American nature studies had passed through four stages; beginning with his diaries, they had flourished next on the green verbiage of his debates with Roberts, then appeared in chrysalid form as review articles, and finally emerged in book form. In 1890 one of these articles was read by R. B. Cunninghame Graham, who wrote to ask whether the writer spoke from experience of the pampas, where he himself had lived for nine years. Cunninghame Graham, known to his friends as Don Roberto, was to become something of a legend in his own lifetime. Of mixed Scottish and Spanish descent, he had already enjoyed a superbly

adventurous career—such a life as Richard Lamb had
led, and as Hudson himself had lost—and would continue to roam the world, to ride, to write and to fight
for many causes: living, as A. F. Tschiffely wrote,
"in the romanticism of a Byron and in the idealism of a
Don Quixote". In later years he was strikingly like
Van Dyck's portrait of Charles I, from whom he could
claim direct descent. As a young man, however, his
photographs closely resemble one of Hudson in his
twenties, the keen eyes, fine features and air of vigour
and sensitive pride being marked in each. He had an
engaging way of creating, in much that he said and
wrote, a kind of order of the knights of pampas and
prairie; and Hudson, whether or not he took the
other quite seriously, was certainly touched and happy
to find himself honoured among the initiate. In dark
moods, when writing was mere painful toil, the plough-
ing of barren rock, and life itself "a burden almost not
to be borne", the younger man could evoke for him
another and a more vital self. In a sense other than the
literal one (although their use of Spanish was clearly
part of the bond between them) they could speak the
same language. And if Morley Roberts helped Hudson
to write as a naturalist, it was Cunninghame Graham
who created for him a climate in which the seed of
his story *El Ombú* stirred and began to unfold in his
thoughts.

Hudson at first was reluctant to accept invitations,
writing artlessly to his new friend: "I could no more
dine at Chester Square with you and your friends
than with Fairies and Angels. These beings do not
really dine, they sup, but let that pass. The fact is,
being poor I long ago gave up going to houses dining.
One of the Apostles, a certain Paul, warned us against

'unequal' alliances, and Aesop touches instructively on the same subject in one of his parables. . . ." But, despite St. Paul and Aesop, he was later often to be found among the writers and artists who met in Chester Square at the house of Cunninghame Graham's mother, the beautiful Mrs. Bontine, who was quick to appreciate his personal charm and the quality of his writing.

Others, too, were becoming aware of that fascination, although they saw that he never fully revealed himself: "a lonely man, even when in congenial company", Coulson Kernahan thought him, while Henry Salt was struck by his likeness to "a great sad raptorial bird", with "deep-set desolate eyes looking through and beyond us". At ease among his friends he could be a brilliant talker and most disarming companion. More often, as time went on, he could escape from the sombre garret of Tower House to happier surroundings: to Chester Square; to the little fishing-cottage on the Itchen lent to him by Sir Edward Grey; once, in 1894, to Ireland; to visit Mrs. Phillips, Mrs. Hubbard and other enthusiasts of the Bird Society, to whom he was like a kind and devoted brother; to meetings of the Humanitarian League, or more light-hearted gatherings of the literary world. At one of these his hostess was an American poet, Louise Chandler Moulton, who with impulsive generosity longed to help him.

"He struck me as such a lonely—almost tragically lonely—man!" she declared after their meeting. "I suspect that for some reason his life is unhappy. If it were only that he is poor, which I also suspect to be the case, one might be privileged to help, but he is, I imagine, intensely proud, and in the case of so sensitive a man, one can't go too carefully where money is concerned. Besides, there is strength, character, determination, written on that gaunt and somewhat grim face, and I can't think that mere money cares account for the loneliness—the soul-loneliness—which is also written there."

Mrs. Moulton was not alone in her concern, nor was hers the only impulse of practical sympathy to be daunted by fear of touching his pride. But now the chorus of voices urging that he should have help and recognition grew more insistent and authoritative. He himself became aware of this, and was persuaded to take the necessary steps toward claiming British citizenship. His naturalization papers were signed in April 1900 in the Zoological Society's rooms in Hanover Square. A month later came the publication of *Nature in Downland*; to be followed by the award of a Civil List pension of £150 a year, "in recognition of the originality of his writings on natural history". Never, perhaps, has any such award returned, to the country that gave it, a richer and more memorable harvest.

CHAPTER VI

A Kingdom to Himself

Hᴇ ᴡᴀs in his sixtieth year; yet for another decade life seemed still to lie before him, various, beautiful and new. In this sunset light, beyond the smoky roofs of Westbourne Park, his horizon widened, and he dared to think again of crossing the Atlantic. Stirred by the enterprise of Cunninghame Graham, who was never content to let journeys remain mere dreams, he wrote: "If I can get up energy enough I may go to America for a few weeks . . . I could visit some relations in New Hampshire and Maine . . ." (His family feeling, and his interest in "our little band" of brothers and sisters, had never diminished; and when, in 1908, the youngest daughter of his sister Mary visited England with her husband, he invited the couple to stay at Tower House, and took great care that they should see as much of London as possible in the three weeks of their visit.) But that year he went no further west than Cornwall. Again, two years later, the voyage was in prospect: "I have made up my mind to go to America for a few weeks, but shall not go if we [Emily and himself] go away soon together—it will be too late at the end of October." It was too late. Then, three years after: "The only place out of England I wish to go to (and hope to go before long) is New England, Maine and New Hampshire and Vermont, where my mother's people are. I have never seen any of them, nor her

native place, and have a wish and desire—a kind of
pious or superstitious feeling—to pay it a visit. It is
the red man's feeling, and I am a red man, or at all
events a wild man of the woods." But after all he was
too ill to go, and always there was a book—and then
another book—for which to save his strength: dreading,
as he started each, that he would not live to finish it.
Often he was too ill to write. Yet at other times his
vitality seemed inexhaustible.

Writing, however, was no longer "that woundy
business" of Galsworthy's description, "long to learn,
hard to learn, and no gift of the angels". He had always
worked at a leisurely pace, correcting and rewriting
with care; though complicating his task by the habit
of drafting his first script on the backs of envelopes
or scraps of paper. These methods did not change:
but now misguided imitation and self-distrust had been
thrown aside, and he was no longer tongue-tied by
the authority of editors. Freedom from money worries
brought mental freedom; nor were country expeditions
now a rarity, to be paid for in scanty dinners and
threadbare clothes, but an exhilarating way of life
which never failed to bring him hope and strength,
"as though I had sloughed off a frayed and rusty en-
velope and come out like a ring-snake in new green
and gold". His pension had made this way of life
secure, but the new confidence had been achieved before
its award: in *Nature in Downland* he had come into his
own, writing with assurance and grace from the
springs of poetic feeling.

This book, in which he brought to perfection the
essay form on which the later country books were
modelled, is self-revealing as any he wrote. In its
freshness, lucid colour, pith and pungency it resembles

the bright wild-flower gardens of the chalk, which delighted him with their medley of delicate small weeds and grasses, blue butterflies, sweet herbs and drunken bees. To the bees, indeed, he showed more tolerance than to the village toper or to the city of Chichester, with its twenty churches and seventy public houses, which he censured in a famous passage. Hudson was writing, however, in a time when drunken labourers were an everyday sight, in a countryside where the farm-hand's job had become degraded and his diet miserable, while only the solace of the inn remained in place of the dead village arts and pastimes. As a rule he loved and sympathised with the country people. One of the most delightful passages in *Nature in Downland* tells of his meeting a fellow-wanderer on the downs near Lewes, whom he found to be also a fellow-prisoner exulting in release—not from London, but from the county gaol. The man's pleasure in his freedom, in the hot sunlight and green turf, his shining face and bunch of yellow flags stuck into his ragged coat, are most feelingly described. "He must indeed have been happy, and seen all familiar things with a strange magical beauty in them." It was in this same glorious mood, from the shades of the prison-house, that he himself saw England.

That passion for freedom gives the book its most painful moment, also, as he tells the story of a white owl imprisoned in a hot, brightly lit kitchen in a Chichester house. Having persuaded the owner to let him set it free, he first searched the neighbourhood to find the perfect surroundings, where it would be watched over until it could again fend for itself; only to be told by the owl's gaoler, on his return, that she had changed her mind. Pleading was in vain. His horror, his helplessness and the rage he felt are expressed in the last few lines of the tale. "I could only try to believe that there is some foundation for the ancient belief held in so many lands, that the owl is indeed a supernatural, or sacred, bird; that when this captive had been tortured to death and its carcass thrown into the dust-heap, the loving-kindness that had been shown to him would have a swift and suitable reward."

The label "unscientific" has become attached to Hudson, and certainly there are times when enthusiasm appears to blind him as well as lesser men. Here he tells, for instance, of a downland shepherd who had had in his flock a lamb born with its face deformed into the likeness of an owl's face: the ewe having been frightened, as the shepherd believed, by coming suddenly upon a long-eared owl perched in a furze bush. The same observant shepherd had known a lamb born with hare's fur, and concluded that the ewe had in that case been startled by a hare. Hudson comments: "What did surprise me was that this man, with only the light of nature to go by, had found the right interpretation of these strange cases." The reader might be surprised in turn—not at his interest in the theory of pre-natal suggestion (then a comparatively new term) but at his acceptance of such evidence. The owl incident was supposed to have taken place "about fifteen years ago"; and the shepherd, warming to his story, had gone on to assert that long-eared owls were then commonly seen in the downland furze patches, although "he believed that the long-eared owl had now forsaken the downs. But though he was so positive about his facts, I am still in doubt as to the species: our memories play strange tricks with all of us at times;

and after all it may have been in the autumn months
that the birds were seen, and that the species was the
world-wandering short-eared owl". Hudson, in fact,
is unwilling to spoil such a tempting deposition by
admitting that a ewe was unlikely to have come face
to face with an owl, long-eared or not. (The shepherd
was on safer ground when he talked of hare's fur.)
Forgetting his old indignation with Messrs. Darwin
and Murphy, he is amusing himself by a little innocent
conjuring with "the truths of nature". When he has
no such bee in his bonnet he can shrug and smile with
any countryman: as, for instance, when he comes on
a dead fox at midsummer in hunting country and
murmurs satirically, "Careless fellow! you have gone
and got yourself bitten by an adder . . ." then adds,
"In spite of hounds and 'adders', the fox continues
only too numerous. . . ."

Despite moments of haunting sadness, as in a passage
on the untimely death of Jefferies, *Nature in Downland* is one of his happiest books. Over so much of his
best work in fiction an immense melancholy shadow
seems to brood; but the sunlight of a memorable
summer shines in this landscape; larks, whitethroats,
linnets and yellowhammers sing from cover to cover,
a coastguard's children bask in brilliant light like
young wild rabbits, a pretty little girl crosses his path
and speaks to him with a voice sweet as a blackbird's,
and when the leaves have fallen the winter beechwoods
stand in the sunset like white columns on a golden
floor. For one individual that infuriates him, there
are always a dozen to gladden his heart: "Beauty and
grace and sweetness and melody—you will find them
here, too, in the shadow of the downs, although not so
frequently as in the sweet west country. Still, my

experience is that the fair to see, and . . . the gracious in mind and manner, are not very rare."

Ten years intervened between the publication of *Nature in Downland* and the essay which is perhaps his most perfect work in this form—*A Shepherd's Life*. During this time four others appeared. In each, the curiosity of the field naturalist, the love of ideas and facts and little oddities, wherever he found them, the hatred of meanness and cruelty and stupidity, make a pattern of light and dark over the essential fabric—the worship of beauty that covered his life as the living garment of turf covers the downs. As in the earlier books, *Idle Days in Patagonia* and *The Naturalist in La Plata*, his experiences as a naturalist are treated from a literary rather than a scientific point of view; but these later essays have at their best an exhilarating and lyrical quality lacking in the immature work. His looks went everywhere, and in the writer's sense he approved all that he saw: if the essays have a major fault, it is lack of discrimination. Yet even here the flaw may lie in the reader's imaginative range; to Hudson, a lame story of a "lady of fashion", moved to tears by a portrait of herself in youth, was perhaps incisive as another that seems to hold all the deadly innocence of Hans Andersen—the tale of a curious friendship between a fish and a solitary swan, and of its pathetic ending. More often he carries the reader with him from the sheer impetus of his own sympathy and vitality.

In *Birds and Man*, however, as it first appeared, in 1901, one is conscious of taking a backward step into the duller period when these papers were written, before he had found himself in the writing of *Downland*. One of the more interesting chapters describes his first visit to Selborne, and his sense of the enduring presence there of Gilbert White; another, "A Secret of the Charm of Flowers", was the outcome of long discussion with Roberts on a favourite idea of Hudson's— that much of this charm was due to human associations. *Birds and Man* was later revised, and among the fresh material added was a little fantasy in his most savage and compelling vein, under the misleading title "Something Pretty in a Glass Case". But in *Hampshire Days*, which followed in 1903, he was writing again in the finely sustained and assured manner of the Sussex essay. With engaging resilience he turns from recording the hour-to-hour history of a young cuckoo in a robin's nest, to an old woman's vigorous lament at the supplanting of elderberry wine and home-made bread by commercial wares. Or, in another mood, he sets down his feelings in sitting by a "mound of the ancient dead" while twilight deepens over the oak woods of Beaulieu: he is serenely conscious that, while the dead might regard with hatred and resentment "the little eager busy people, hateful in their artificial indoor lives", he himself is accepted and at one with them.

In the summer of 1901 he had eagerly awaited the verdict on another manuscript, sent to the firm of Heinemann. This contained two long stories, *El Ombú* and *Marta Riquelme*, and two shorter ones. *El Ombú*, which was to give the book its name, has been described as one of the best short stories ever written in English. The story-teller is Nicandro, "that old man to whom we all loved to listen", and in his person Hudson unfolds with grave simplicity the terrible story of a doomed house and its inhabitants. As with *Marta Riquelme*, and later in the ending of *Green Mansions*, sheer anguish is the keynote. As the reader interprets

for himself the old gaucho's matter-of-fact recital, the
effect produced is that of the Greek tragic pattern—
intensity of feeling, mounting tension, a dreadful and
irrevocable climax, and frenzy dying away in the quiet
anti-climax. The height of the story is reached when
the monstrous General Barboza, a man like an eagle—
"that great bird that has no weakness and no mercy . . .
whose pleasure it is to tear his victim's flesh with his
crooked talons"—is advised to bathe in the carcass of
a freshly-killed bull as a cure for some obscure disease.
From this terrible blood bath he leaps naked and raving
mad, to hurl himself at his assembled soldiers, "yelling
and whirling his sword round so that it looked like a
shining wheel in the sun": then falls dead. In *Marta
Riquelme* the narrative is more strained: the story of a
woman's sufferings and losses being told by a Jesuit
priest in love with the unhappy Marta, and torn alike
by his pity for her and by his own religious struggle.
The climax is reached in her disappearance and supposed transformation into the dreaded Kakué bird,
that shrieked in the Jujuy forest with a voice like a
human cry, "yet expressing a degree of agony and
despair surpassing the power of any human soul to
feel".

Whether or not the reader can endure the atmosphere
of these stories, the sense of bloodshed in brilliant sunlight that permeates *El Ombú*, and the hysterical stress
on darkness and degradation in *Marta Riquelme*, there
is no denying their sustained inspiration and imaginative power. Heinemann's reader, Edward Garnett,
declared that *El Ombú* was a work of genius and must
be published. On the September morning when Hudson
called to learn of his decision, Garnett told him that
he had written a masterpiece: at which Hudson (as he

recalled) "glared at me as if he would annihilate me". The reader had, in his own words, been swept off his feet by its grave beauty and tragic sweetness: a phrase which may be felt to describe more aptly the haunting charm of Hudson's best-known story, *Green Mansions*.

The friendship with Edward Garnett, begun that morning in the publisher's office, prospered; and David Garnett has explained that it was his father's influence and encouragement which led Hudson to finish this long-cherished but neglected manuscript. To Morley Roberts, who had heard him speak of it years before, this story bore the stamp of the treasured project which the author can never bring himself even to begin; and when at last he read the finished book it seemed to bear little relation to that story which had been coloured for him, over the years, by Hudson's words and his tone of voice. Between the dream and the reality, the image of Rima and the written page, had fallen a shadow deeper than the disparity which must always exist. The construction of the tale is at fault; yet so powerful is the image that even this clumsiness cannot dispel its magic.

The green mansions are the trees of the great Venezuelan forest that Hudson had never seen, but whose mysterious wild paradise is painted, fern by fern, leaf by leaf, shadow on shadow, through the eyes of the hero Abel. Day after day, as he wanders in the forest, he hears a strange warbling in the tree-tops, like the voice of a bird, yet also curiously like a human voice. He discovers that his Indian guide is terrified of this voice, which the Indians believe to be that of "the daughter of the Didi", a malicious forest spirit. At length he meets an old man, Nuflo, who lives in a hut in the forest, and finds that the voice is that of his grandchild Rima. The Indians of the region had, in her childhood, been friendly to herself and to Nuflo: ". . . but when Rima grew up, developing into that mysterious woodland girl I found her, they became suspicious, and in the end regarded her with dangerously hostile feeling. She, poor child, detested them because they were incessantly at war with the wild animals she loved, her companions; and having no fear of them, for she did not know that they had it in their minds to turn their little poisonous arrows against herself, she was constantly in the woods frustrating them."

Abel and Rima are in love: but during a brief separation tragedy intervenes. The Indian describes her end to Abel, the hunters having trapped her in a tree. "While the men cut and brought great trees, the women and children gathered dry stuff in the forest and brought it in their arms and piled it round. Then they set fire to it on all sides, laughing and shouting, 'Burn, burn, daughter of the Didi!' At length all the lower branches of the big tree were on fire, and the trunk was on fire, but above it was still green, and we could see nothing. But the flames went up higher and higher with a great noise; and at last from the top of the tree, out of the green leaves, came a great cry, like the cry of a bird, 'Abel! Abel!' and then looking we saw something fall; through leaves and smoke and flame it fell like a great white bird killed with an arrow and falling to the earth, and fell into the flames beneath. And it was the daughter of the Didi, and she was burnt to ashes like a moth in the flames of a fire, and no one has ever heard or seen her since."

Whether read as romance or poignant metaphor, *Green Mansions* is like no other tale; it pierces the heart;

and it is unforgettable. As a writer on natural history
and the countryside Hudson was already established;
but with this book and the revised version of *The Purple
Land*, both published in 1904, he reached a far wider
circle of readers in England and in America. The
"handfuls of gold" remained modest, but unqualified
success and even fame (to his somewhat bitter amusement) were now his.

But, if he cared little for this belated success, he
still valued highly the friends that it brought him. His
chief pleasures when in London were now a weekly
luncheon at the Mont Blanc restaurant, and the gatherings of his friends on Wednesday afternoons at Tower
House. At the Mont Blanc, under the influence of
Edward Garnett, a circle of younger writers would
meet; this included Edward Thomas, Walter de la
Mare, R. A. Scott James, W. H. Davies, Hilaire Belloc,
Ford Madox Hueffer, and sometimes John Galsworthy
and Joseph Conrad.

Edward Thomas he loved: this was the son he
should have had, if (in Jefferies' wry phrase) everything did not happen in the Turkish manner. When
Thomas wrote his *Richard Jefferies* he asked Hudson
if he might dedicate the book to him, declaring, "It
gave me such pleasure even to think of connecting the
book with you that I had to speak of it." Of the deep
intimacy between them Mrs. Helen Thomas has written:
"He and Edward constantly wrote to each other and
met often in London. Edward responded to this somewhat austere, solitary man, and honoured him above
all writers of the time." Their tastes in literature
were often the same; each loved *The Anatomy of
Melancholy*. Both were mystics. And how profoundly
Hudson understood Thomas is shown in a letter written

to Edward Garnett, in which he criticises Thomas's *Happy-Go-Lucky-Morgans* and adds: "I believe he has taken the wrong path and is wandering lost in the vast wilderness. He is essentially a poet, one would say of the Celtic variety. . . . I should say that in his nature books and fiction he leaves all there's best and greatest in him unexpressed. . . . I believe that if Thomas had the courage or the opportunity to follow his own genius he could do better things than these."

This verdict was to be ironically fulfilled when, in the war years, Thomas found his short-lived opportunity. Hudson, with Edward Garnett, was then one of the few to be shown his first poems. Hudson's sympathy and perceptiveness, however, did not extend to appreciation of the poems when published. He actually wrote (in 1919): "I had a thin volume of verses by Edward Thomas sent to me a few days ago but find his poetic gift was a rather small one." Against this insensitive verdict, however, one must place Hudson's admiration for Charles Doughty's massive epic, *The Dawn in Britain*, which had, he admitted, impaired his taste for "smoother" kinds of verse. This work has something of the sombre atmosphere of his own story of Saxon England, *Dead Man's Plack*: it has an air very unlike the bloomy wind of Thomas's poetry, with its simple imagery, its "gold and gossamer like a dandelion", the green road strewn with white goose feathers, or the tender starlit night where

> Out in the dark over the snow
> The fallow fawns invisible go
> With the fallow doe. . . .

Yet these very qualities of Thomas's imagination drew Hudson to him with a feeling of warmth never expressed until Hudson's first meeting with Mrs. Thomas, a few days before Hudson's own death.

On his friends Hudson made a profound impression. His striking appearance, his gentle manners, his magnetism, his air of loneliness, are over and over again recorded. " His peculiar mysterious charm was indescribable," wrote Sir William Rothenstein, who in 1906 painted the portrait of him which hangs in the National Gallery. "Something about him tore at one's heart, so loveable he was. Yet he never invited affection: he was a lonely man, with something of the animal about him, walking away and returning with the non-chalance of an animal, and then disappearing again." Others noted his lithe walk, like that of an athlete, "a reserve of power and scorn that was impressive", and qualities of beauty and harmony blending with a deeper strain of passion and melancholy. His beauty, Violet Hunt declared, was in his whole being, not only in his face, which to her seemed "too small, too beak-like, too much refined to a point. If, as we have it," her perceptive account continues, "all men suggest likeness to some animal, one might figure him some bird pressing forward against a gale; his profile and his hair, even, had a wind-blown, backward sweep. It was not an open face, the gaze of it was, on the whole, too shrewd, too wilful and withdrawn. The eyes were bright and dark, the regard narrowed continually in a sort of wild, astute vigilance": the same vigilance that Richard Curle saw in him as they watched wild geese together in Norfolk. He noted, too, the look of coldness, "covering, maybe, a boiling indignation", with which Hudson examined a dead goose shot by a wild-fowler; and the keen glance that was like that of a Red Indian, while he gazed through the trees at grebes swimming on a lake, "as though he could never gaze enough". So absorbed and passionate was that gaze that his companion, feeling suddenly an intruder, withdrew and left him, as long ago his mother had left him, alone in his still ecstasy.

Children loved him, and he treated them gently and with courtesy, knowing that it was often from the very young rather than from their elders that he could learn something new and interesting. In 1905 he published a story for children, *A Little Boy Lost*. But, egoist as he was, he would not simulate polite interest. He could be extremely brusque, for instance, with mothers when they reproached him for ignoring their little girls once these had passed the age of childish originality. Sometimes, when invited to visit a friend, he would ask with quite unconscious rudeness, "Who will be there?" It was as though he heard always the wings of Time, and feared to waste an hour. Of his experiences in Worthing, where he later became a frequent visitor, he wrote with ingenuous disgust: "I have never yet met anyone in it who has been of any use to me. It is talk, talk, talk, but never a gleam of an original or fresh remark or view of anything that does not come out of a book and newspaper." He did not suffer the fool gladly. Of one elegant young poet of the Yellow Book period he wrote savagely: "He comes to you, as it were, fresh from the dressing-table, with all the cosmetics, powders and perfumes on him. One would like to kick him." Publishers were often targets for displeasure—"champion swindlers of the trade" was one of his milder dicta on a firm with whom he dealt—and his criticisms of books could be equally merciless. With increasing years, too, his stock of patience and tolerance dwindled. Yet his was too spacious a personality, "generous, guiltless and of free disposition", to admit malice in a narrow sense. His gaucho companions had taught him, from the time he was six years old, to give hard knocks in return for those received, rather than to turn the other cheek. H. J. Massingham found in him "an almost Miltonic severity: his dignity and reticence were such as men used to associate with the nobleman, and a man so full of character, so solitary and aloof and a kingdom to himself, might well give the impression of being roughened by prejudice and hardly approachable. He did indeed take some knowing . . . some navigating his numerous but agreeably salty prejudices. But once over the bar and his friend, one found a person-ality that was gracious and affectionate, if melancholy and a little lacking in humour". Here, however, Edward Garnett understood him better: "It was necessary to have a sense of *his* humour. And certain people failed to recognize it because it was very deep." Obviously there was laughter behind such an irritable outburst as his defence of Conservatism: "Progress means slaught-ering birds and cutting down woods to build beastly rabbit-hutches for people to breed boys to rob nests."

Women, Edward Garnett records, felt instinctively his immediate responsiveness to their grace and charm. Some writers have suggested that he was an ascetic, wholly absorbed in Nature and indifferent to them; an opinion easily formed from his habit of reticence, but nevertheless absurd, as Morley Roberts made clear, and as letters remain to confirm. Toward the end of his life he began to feel a deep distaste at the thought that after his death "the curiosity of the mean scandal-loving world", with its "insatiable appetite for personal 'revelations' ", might seize on such letters, treasured by women friends, and he wished them to be destroyed. He felt that in his books he had given the world much, and that the world (or that part of it which would not care two straws for his books) might fairly be asked to leave his private life alone. Yet few people have inspired more admiration and affection than he; and, while his stronger instinct was for privacy, in some moods he could take a more defiant (though still a defensive) view. To one friend he wrote: "Do you know the old lines, 'Time, the old god, invests all things with honour and makes them white'? For me, and I hope for you, time is not needed, nor clear reason, nor intuition, which reveals the hidden true meaning and the right and wrong of things, to know that it is good to meet you, to invest our relations with honour and make our lives white. And if in a score or fifty years' time others could know this secret of ours, they would say of it—what do you think? They would say that my friendship with you—and more than friendship—was the sweetest and best and most purifying influence I had known, and that because of it I was better as well as infinitely happier."

It was after he had finished *Hampshire Days* that Morley Roberts persuaded him to pay his first visit to Cornwall, and he found himself—perhaps because of the Irish strain in his breeding—at home on this wild sea-coast and among this dark Celtic type of people. Sea, sky, air, earth, the golden furze and the wild life of the moors drew him back again and again for long visits; and eventually the county became a second home to him. Yet there were points in the Cornish character and way of life that he found far from admirable. His book *The Land's End*, published in 1908, holds the essence of these Cornish days, but was not the idyllic account which some Cornishmen would have preferred to read. In particular, his denunciation of the practice of bird-taking with fish-hooks, then in use at St. Ives, raised a storm which delighted the coat-trailing streak in him, so that he wrote with an audible chuckle: "The St. Ives people are very angry with me for exposing their bird-tor-turing practices. . . . I'm very glad they are angry: perhaps they will now mend their ways a little." Soon afterward he received an invitation from a literary society in Camborne to justify in person his "charges" against Cornishmen, and the anxious Morley Roberts had to beg him on no account to make himself a target for a "rough mining population" which felt itself insulted.

The following year came another country essay, *Afoot in England*, describing many of his encounters and reflections in that "sweet west country" which he preferred to any part of England. The pace is uneven, but the book has unfailing interest and some out-standing passages; notably a chapter "On Going Back", where the reader seems to stray with Hudson into an atmosphere indescribably sinister and grotesque, like the setting for a ghost story told by Dr. M. R. James's "Antiquary".

There followed in 1910 his masterpiece among the country essays: *A Shepherd's Life*. Here there is no unevenness, either in style or matter, but pastoral history set down with quiet simplicity in prose of the highest order. Hudson calls his shepherd Caleb Bawcombe, of Winterbourne Bishop; his actual name was James Lawes, and his home Martin, near Salis-bury, a village which Hudson greatly loved. The names of these chapters—"The Deer-Stealers", "The

Shepherd as Naturalist", "The Shepherd on Foxes", "Shepherds and Poaching", "A Sheep-dog's Life"—indicate the unique quality and richness of the book, with its vast and intimate learning in the life of this west downland countryside. Squires, farmers, game-keepers, villagers and gypsies take their part in the pattern; there is a beautiful description of the valley of the chalk-stream, the Wylye, with its manor-houses, churches and tiny villages, wild flowers and cottage garden flowers, "so old that they have entered the soul"; and, as with all the essays, *A Shepherd's Life* is inlaid with exquisite short stories. Its supreme value (particularly in the two chapters on "Old Wiltshire Days") lies in the fact that it forms a link between "living memory", as it existed in 1909 in these villages, and the newspaper files and legal records from which Hudson verified the grim stories he heard of those old days. How remote seem the times when a young out-of-work farm labourer could be hanged for stealing a sheep to feed his starving family! but Hudson talked to two old people, one aged eighty-nine, the other ninety-three, who well remembered the unfortunate widow and her three children. It was from this tale, now scarcely credible in the callous disregard it shows for the sufferings of the poor and obscure, that Hudson drew his facts for a strange and impressive short story, *An Old Thorn*. Yet it is clear that, despite their hardships, these Wiltshire people were men and women of character, still conscious of their ancient standing as "the commons of England", and that they had kept this sturdy disposition. The book is dominated by the personality of the shepherd Caleb, who possessed a certain spirit and philosophy found in no other trade. His way of life, as he himself realised, linked him with the men of the Old Testament: and in his last words may be heard the authentic echo of that shepherd-poet who dreamed of finding "abundance of peace, so long as the moon endureth". The old man told Hudson: "I don't say that I want to have my life again, because 'twould be sinful. We must take what is sent. But if 'twas offered to me and I was told to choose my work, I'd say, Give me my Wiltsheer Downs again and let me be a shepherd there all my life long."

CHAPTER VII

The Time Remaining

A SHEPHERD'S LIFE met with instant appreciation; and this, perhaps, gave Hudson more pleasure than he professed to feel. But, for the next few years, he was to find little health or happiness. In the autumn of 1911 Emily Hudson, now over eighty, became seriously ill.

Prosperity had not increased poor Mrs. Hudson's happiness. Failing health had for some years made her dread those periods of loneliness when her husband was walking or cycling about the countryside; also, she found the gatherings of his friends at Tower House trying, and did not always hide her antipathies. She had little in common with these people, and to Morley Roberts would sometimes confide a wish for the return of the old days when "Will" had seemed to depend on her alone. After one of these tea-parties, when the atmosphere had been more strained and unhappy than usual, Hudson accompanied to the door a woman guest who burst into tears and exclaimed passionately, "Why do you stay here? Why don't you find someone to love, and go away?" Herself happily married, she was utterly taken aback by the quiet desperation of his answer: "Oh, I have loved you for years. *For years.*"

But more and more, as time went on, the Hudsons' relationship had tended to become reversed, and now it was Emily who depended on her husband. This illness made her far more nervous and exacting than before. She could not bear to be left, even for an hour; and, imprisoned in this distressing situation, his own health began to break down. The "stammering heart" and other ills which he had carried for years became a heavy burden, and, although he said little of this to others, the change in his spirit and outlook was marked. Emily Hudson recovered, but she was now bedridden, and at length in April 1914 he accompanied her to Worthing "in the hope", as he wrote compassionately, "of finding somewhere where she could exist without me". Sympathising with her dread of nursing-homes, he found her rooms in a guest-house where she lived with a companion for the next three years, consoled in his absence by his frequent letters. He himself could no longer face the summer heat or winter fog of London; and most of his time was spent at Worthing, at Grey Friars (a country house near Ascot, lent to him by one of his closest friends, Margaret Ranee of Sarawak) or in Cornwall. From Lelant, where he had also gone as the Ranee's guest, he wrote wistfully to Cunninghame Graham in South America, "How I envy you all those wanderings and adventurings you must have had! And now you talk of Venezuela!"—while he, then struggling up from a three months' illness, could scarcely hope to reach Land's End or Godolphin. The fact that his latest essay *Adventures Among Birds* had been highly praised, that his books were now in demand before they were written, and that American publishers were competing in their eagerness to bring out new editions of *The Purple Land* and *A Crystal Age*, gave him little satisfaction and seemed only a source of weariness. "It would amuse me very much," he wrote, "if the sudden popularity had not come so late in the day."

The war, which one historian has called "that vastest disordering since the breakdown of the Pax Romana", remained for him unrealised. At its outbreak he wrote carelessly: "I think it is a blessed war, and it was quite time we had one for purification . . . from the degeneration, the rottenness that comes of everlasting peace. . . . The blood that is being shed will purge us of many hateful qualities." Such illusions were, after all, common in 1914, though perhaps their expression was appropriate only in the fighting man: and by him soon abandoned in the light of reality. Hudson suffered at the loss of such young men as Edward Thomas and Rupert Brooke, just as he suffered later at the news of the death of his younger sister, Mary Ellen, in Buenos Aires. But this was not his war. He was too old, too ill, and there were books clamouring to be written which he could scarcely hope to write.

His long illness in the winter of 1915–16, when after catching a chill he lay for three months in a Cornish convent hospital, brought him a strange and radiant experience. He had been reading Serge Aksakoff's *History of My Childhood*; and this, combined with his weak state, and with the sound of the winter storm outside the window, seemed to lull him into a kind of waking trance in which he relived his childhood, feeling himself thousands of miles away in the sun and wind of the pampas. Pencil in hand, he began at once to write down some of these revelations; and this story, which he called *Far Away and Long Ago*, grew into an achievement complete and perfect in its visionary quality and lucid simplicity of writing.

The summer of 1916 found him back at Tower House, absorbed in work, cared for by a housekeeper, and going as often as possible to visit Emily Hudson at

Worthing. He was busy with articles, the auto-biography, and the revision of *Birds in a Village* and other early books for new editions; and his adventurous mind had already begun coursing after a hundred fresh ideas (started by the impact of those early experiences and impressions) later to be crystallised into a book on "the seventeen or twenty senses we are endowed with". But now the legacy of heart weakness, left by his boyhood attack of rheumatic fever, entered a new and grave phase. Morley Roberts, who had studied cardiology and who watched unobtrusively over his friend's health, recognised this change and sent him to a specialist. Told that he must not expect his health ever to be right again, he was given digitalis and instructions how to use it, and warned of the danger of bronchial attacks. This did not prevent his getting up in the middle of the night, during an air raid, and going into the street in the hope of seeing a Zeppelin; but life was sweet to him and he learned to walk warily and to give up, at last, even those claims on his pity which hitherto had taken the first place in his life. "I want to use whatever time remains to me in doing my own work," he wrote to Edward Garnett. "The world is a shambles, but I wasn't born to set it right."

Yet, though he would no longer intervene directly in cases of cruelty—as in that of a chained owl, which must have reminded him painfully of his old defeat in trying to save the owl at Chichester—the welfare of the Bird Protection Society was still his first concern. He meant to leave whatever money he had to further its work; and, with this aim, he drove hard bargains with publishers over his new books, and, careless of his hard-won reputation, consented to the publication in book form of *Ralph Herne* and the reissue of *Fan*, though knowing how slight was their true value. He was eager, also, to sell his first editions at high prices for this cause; yet he could be curiously blind to financial values, and, although parts of his later manuscripts were saved—including some chapters of *Far Away and Long Ago*, the story *Dead Man's Plack*, and *A Shepherd's Life*, which he gave to Lady Rothenstein—many more were sacrificed to the passion for destroying papers and letters which now possessed him at intervals.

The strenuous country rambles, the long cycle rides, the days of bird-watching in woods or on open marshlands in all weathers—these had at last been left behind. The best he could hope for in their stead was to sit under a cedar tree in a Surrey park and listen to the nightingale. Outwardly his life settled into a quiet rhythm, the winters being passed in lodgings at 23 North Parade, Penzance, the summer and autumn months in London. Throughout the winter of 1917, and on through another summer and another winter, the writing of *Far Away and Long Ago* continued. In Penzance, while he sat by his fireside, storms swept in from the bay and seagulls cried; in London, traffic roared and sparrows chirped outside the summer gloom of Tower House; but he was not there to hear them. In the few working hours that now made up his real life, he returned day after day to his vision of the pampas. He saw the great flocks of birds, the brilliant flowers, the snakes, the moonlit trees; he felt again that childish urge toward nature-worship which all his life, save in the tortured years of adolescence, had meant more to him than any orthodox religion; he remembered his father and mother, his brothers and sisters, and the laughter of his youth. Grimly taking his supper of boiled milk and bread, he smiled to himself as he recalled those "past perilous adventures" of eating that had pleased his boyish appetite: the hot maize-meal cakes and syrup on which he had break-fasted, or the salad of cold sliced potatoes and onions, drenched in oil and vinegar, "a glorious dish with cold meat to go to bed on!" He painted gay and spirited pictures, a little larger than life, of neighbours on the plain; and another, gentle and shadowy, of the little girl who had possessed his childish love, and whom he had never forgotten. With such inspiration, such rich memories and patient craftsmanship, such gratitude and love of life to enlighten his tranquillity, it was little wonder that he produced a masterpiece in that thorny and crowded field of childhood memoirs.

The book was published in the autumn of 1918, and the praise it received from reviewers might have seemed overwhelming to a writer less implacably determined not to be impressed. Still perversely loyal to the half-starved aspirant whom he had remained for nearly thirty years, he assured Edward Garnett, "All those twenty or thirty columns of it I've seen so far had not one thought in it all to give me any pleasure." He knew that the praise was deserved, yet he insisted that it came too late to have any meaning for him, refusing to admit that it can rarely be given to any creative artist to have youth and fame together. Always he felt that time was desperately short, while his powers of mind were undiminished: so he growled at professional applause and went doggedly on with new work. His essays were in constant demand by editors, and in 1919 there appeared a new collection, *The Book of a Naturalist*. This included all that he had written of his abandoned *Book of the Serpent*, condensed into four brilliant chapters. He had begun to write *Dead Man's Plack*: a task which he found wearisome because it was out of character, yet one which he felt impelled to finish. He had also to revise his two hundred descriptive passages from *Argentine Ornithology*, to be reprinted as *Birds of La Plata*, and to supervise the drawing of the coloured plates with which it was illustrated. But the work which most absorbed him was the long essay on the senses, eventually called *A Hind in Richmond Park*, and to this (as his custom was in writing) he returned again and again, as his mood dictated. In this discursive essay, facts, speculations, discussion, and illustration are woven loosely into a fabric of great beauty and interest. Beginning with an incident in Richmond Park, when he had kept watch on a hind as she lay listening to woodland sounds too faint for his own hearing, he moves forward to consider various faculties in animals and human beings in the light of a lifetime's experiences. Following the story of his boyhood, it seems natural that this book should have much in common with his earliest work as a naturalist in *La Plata* and in *Idle Days in Patagonia*. Its atmosphere of "summing-up", also, together with a wide range and awareness of maturity, recall Jefferies' *Amaryllis at the Fair*. Many of its arguments, as in those first works, were discussed in letters exchanged with Morley Roberts; for he could still find time and energy to write long letters, showing how varied his interests remained, how keen his sense of beauty, and how lively and caustic his judgments. Still, too, he loved company, and in London would constantly meet old friends—Roberts, Wilfred Scawen Blunt, the Rothensteins, the Galsworthys, Violet Hunt,

Rabindranath Tagore; while his new friends among the young included Wilfred Ewart, author of a celebrated war book, and Col. Lawrence, who shared his admiration for Charles Doughty.

In Cornwall, also, he enjoyed talking with writers, newspapermen and painters; and it was while returning from a gathering of friends in Penzance, one night in December 1920, that he met with an accident which might well have killed him outright. Missing his footing in the dark, he fell four feet from a pavement into the road, and, though a bruised knee, a gashed hand and sprained wrist were his only outward injuries, he was badly shaken. He could not sleep; sitting up one night by candlelight, he seemed to feel his heart tumbling crazily about in his body, and told himself that he would be found dead in the morning. A few days later he was out again, buying books as Christmas presents for child friends; and, as Roberts saw with affectionate amusement, betraying pleasure at the sight of his own books displayed in the shop. He tried to resume work, and to answer the many letters which came to him almost daily from all over the world; typical of his courtesy in this matter is a letter which he wrote the week after his accident, giving a correspondent minute directions for finding wild columbines in a wood near Salisbury, and explaining in a brief postscript that his handwriting is "worse to read than ever" as his right hand has been hurt. But the new year came in, and he was not well. He was worried, too, by grave reports about Emily, who had become a helpless invalid and now lived with a nurse at West Tarring. In March he was warned that she was unconscious and sinking; but his doctor would not allow him to travel, and a few days later she was dead.

She was buried in Broadwater cemetery at Worthing, where Richard Jefferies also lies, and in June he went to visit the place. "—I wished," he wrote, "that the grave could have been acquired in that part where Jefferies was buried. It is the loveliest spot, with old stone pines and a wealth of flowers and wild plants. But . . . I must be satisfied to rest, as they call it, in a less attractive spot. However, there is a good pine tree by the grave, and the turtle doves were crooning all the time I stayed there. The whole place seemed swarming with birds." He arranged for the plot to be planted thickly with daisies, and a stone placed there on which—perhaps in simplicity, perhaps in irony—he had had engraved the words *I will not fail thee*.

Perhaps this epitaph was in irony: for he hated the thought of death. Even in his worst moments, he had felt always that it was better to be than not to be. He disliked one of Rothenstein's drawings because he felt that it accentuated the lines in his face; and in earlier years he had darkened his greying hair to avoid comment on his age. Now his work had to be set aside while a new will was made, leaving everything to the Bird Protection Society. (His Civil List pension he had resigned, too proud to accept an award of which he was no longer in need.) Yet it was in no spirit of resignation that he put his affairs in order. All his grief for himself and for humanity, doomed to be torn away from the world he loved, went into his essay "The Return of the Chiff-chaff", published that autumn in a last collection, *A Traveller in Little Things*. He dismissed with scorn the trite consolation of those who, never having lived in his sense of the word, could look on death as a deliverer; but among friends he

would persistently and wistfully discuss the chances
of personal immortality. The balance of evidence, he
felt, was on the side of "immortality in the race by
transmitted influence", but not of personal survival
after death: so, for all his grim realism, he may in
private have been comforted by the romantic defiance
of the poet:

> He does not die who can bequeath
> Some influence to the land he knows,
> Or dares, persistent, interwreath
> Love permanent with the wild hedgerows:
> He does not die, but still remains
> Substantiate with his darling plains. . . .[1]

Before returning to Penzance in November he had
carried out another wholesale burning of papers and
letters. He did not expect to see Tower House again.
Yet in the following June, after a long slow winter's
work at *A Hind in Richmond Park*, he was there once
more, living in a single room on the ground floor.
The book was almost finished; but there were other
claims on his time and strength—friends, in London
and Sussex and at Ascot, whom he longed to see, a
present to be bought for a child in Penzance, new
books to be read, appeals for help to be answered. To
Linda Gardiner he wrote in August: "I have lost all
hope of ever getting out of London. Illness, illness
all the time and a perpetual struggle to finish work. . . ."
One service there was—to his dead friend Edward
Thomas—which he would not leave undone. Mrs.
Thomas had asked him to write a preface for *Cloud
Castle*, a posthumous collection of her husband's essays;
and he wrote asking her to lunch with him at White-

[1] Hilaire Belloc.

ley's: "I found him there—a tall gaunt eagle-eyed man who talked only about Edward. He was in tears all the time and said, 'I can't get over his loss. He was as dear to me as if he had been my son. I never had a son, but he, I felt, was the son I would have liked to have, and I loved him. I have no one else, all my love was for him.' He could not speak for weeping. I was too deeply moved to speak. He then asked about my circumstances and said that he had heard they were difficult for me. He said, 'I have first editions of all my books and these are of some value. I will send them to you.' And so we talked for about an hour and he said, 'I should have met you before. It would have been good to talk to you. I am a very ill man and I have not long to live. We shall not meet again.' "

The effort had come too late. The books were never sent. But, in the few days that remained, he managed to draft a preface for *Cloud Castle*, knowing that his name would help to sell the book. It may be that he felt less lonely in the face of death as he forged this last slender link with his "son"; but his instinct, like that of a wild creature, was to die alone. On August 17th, Morley Roberts found him in bed, unable to write and in pain. "He looked so splendid, kind and anxious, and ready, just a little, a very little, to cling not only to life but to one who loved him." Yet Roberts dared not insist on staying. Next morning the housekeeper sent her little girl to his room with his letters; the child returned saying that he was asleep, that she had touched him and he did not wake. On a table at the foot of his bed lay his scattered notes for the last pages of *A Hind in Richmond Park* and the *Cloud Castle* essay.

Had I but time—as this fell sergeant death
Is strict in his arrest—O, I could tell you—
But let it be.

He was buried beside Emily Hudson: but Morley Roberts, who folded his hands as he lay dead, wrote afterwards: "I wished to take him out upon the open pampa, with a long wide view beyond the sight of man even on horseback, and with the great clear sky above. So I would have digged a grave and put him there to rest in his blanket just as he had fallen asleep, without disturbing his attitude of quiet peace."

Bibliography

The Collected Works of W. H. Hudson in 24 volumes. Dent. 1923.

A Hudson Anthology, ed. by Edward Garnett. Dent. 1924.

Men, Books and Birds. Letters to Morley Roberts. Nash & Grayson. 1925.

Letters to R. B. Cunninghame Graham, ed. by Richard Curle. Golden Cockerel Press. 1941.

Letters to Edward Garnett, with an Introduction by Edward Garnett. The Nonesuch Press. 1923.

Letters on the Ornithology of Buenos Ayres, ed. by David R. Dewar. Cornell University Press. 1951.

Pamphlets and Monographs: mainly on behalf of the (Royal) Society for the Protection of Birds and the Humane League.

Poems, articles and *stories* in various periodicals. 1874–1922.

Collected unpublished letters to Mrs. W. H. Hudson, Lady (Alice) Rothenstein, Mrs. Hubbard, Mrs. Phillips, Miss Linda Gardiner, Mrs. Shepherd.

Prefaces to *The Great Deserts and Forests of North America*, by Paul Fountain. Longmans. 1901; and *Cloud Castle and Other Papers* by Edward Thomas. Duckworth. 1922.

W. H. Hudson: A Portrait, by Morley Roberts. Nash & Grayson. 1924.

W. H. Hudson: The Vision of Earth, by Robert Hamilton. Dent. 1946.

W. H. Hudson's Lost Years, by R. Gordon Wasson and Edwin Way Teale. "The Times Literary Supplement." April 1947.

Annual Reports of the Smithsonian Institution of Washington. 1866–69.

Proceedings of the Zoological Society of London. 1869–76.

William Henry Hudson: A Tribute, by various writers, ed. by Samuel J. Looker. Worthing Cavalcade Series. Worthing, Aldridge Bros. 1947.

Edward Thomas's Letters to W. H. Hudson, ed. by James Guthrie. "The London Mercury." August. 1920.

The G. M. Adams-W. H. Hudson Collection, by Carlton F. Wells. University of Michigan. 1943.

Bibliography of the Writings of W. H. Hudson, by G. F. Wilson. "The Bookman's Journal." 1922.

W. H. Hudson's Reading, by H. F. West. Privately printed. 1947.

In translation:

El Mundo Maravilloso de Guillermo Enrique Hudson, by Ezequiel Martinez Estrada. Fondo de Cultura Economica, Mexico. 1951.

Semblanza de Hudson, by Dr. Fernando Pozzo. Instituto de Conferencias del Banco Municipal, Buenos Aires. 1940.

William Henry Hudson, y su Amor A Los Pajaros, by Jorge Casares. Establecimiento Grafico Tomas Palumbo, Buenos Aires. 1930.

The Friendship Between W. H. Hudson and Cunninghame Graham, trans. by José Luís Lanuza from an article in "Acquí Está," Buenos Aires.

Hudson, Naturaleza e Infancia, by Fryda Schultz de Mantovani. Prize essay. "Sur." May 1951.

Hudson Vuelve, by Luis Horacio Velazquez. Buenos Aires. 1952.

The Voyage of a Naturalist, by Charles Darwin. Murray. 1845.

The Paraña and South American Recollections, by Thomas J. Hutchinson. 1868.

The Times Book on Argentina. 1927.

Articles and correspondence in various periodicals, 1917–51, by Edward Garnett, A. Colton, H. J. Massingham, Ernest Rhys, Richard Curle, Philip Gosse, R. B. Cunninghame Graham, R. L. Megroz, Violet Hunt, George Sampson,

M. Y. Hughes, E. M. Nicholson, Roger Fry, Henry S. Salt, Morley Roberts, William Rothenstein, John Galsworthy, J. V. Fletcher, Coulson Kernahan, Ford Madox Heuffer, Robert Hamilton, E. L. Woodward, E. H. L. Poole, W. J. Hemp, V. Sackville-West (broadcast talk), David Garnett.

Books containing references to W. H. Hudson:

A Literary pilgrim in England, by Edward Thomas. Methuen. 1917.

Untrodden Ways, by H. J. Massingham. Unwin. 1923.

The Flurried Years, by Violet Hunt. Hurst & Blackett. 1926.

Spirit of Delight, by G. M. Harper. Benn. 1928.

Birds of Wing and Other Wild Things, by H. F. B. Fox. Dent. 1930.

Men and Memories, by William Rothenstein. Faber & Faber. 1932.

To the Memory of Edward Thomas, by James Guthrie. Pear Tree Press. 1937.

Edward Thomas, by Robert P. Eckert. Dent. 1937.

Autobiography, by Frank Swinnerton. Hutchinson. 1937.

Grey of Fallodon, by G. M. Trevelyan. Longmans. 1937.

Travellers' Rest, by Philip Gosse. Cassell. 1937.

Mightier than the Sword, by Ford Madox Ford (Hueffer). Allen & Unwin. 1938.

Life and Letters of Edward Thomas, by John Moore. Heinemann. 1939.